Surveying the social world

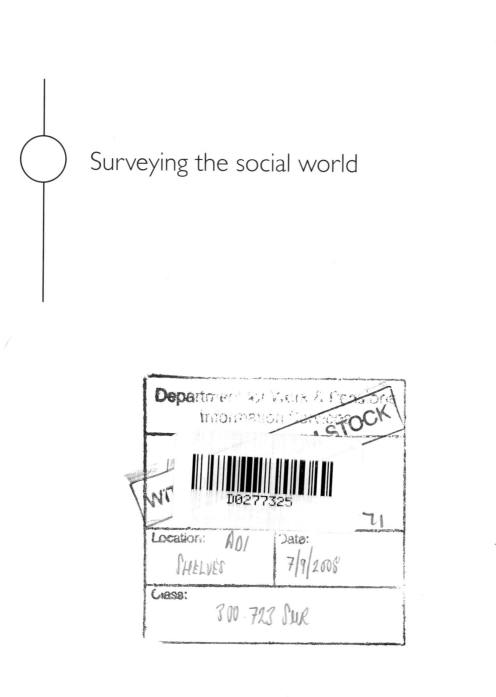

Understanding Social Research

Series Editor: Alan Bryman

Published titles

Surveying the social world

PRINCIPLES AND PRACTICE IN
SURVEY RESEARCH

ALAN ALDRIDGE and KEN LEVINE

Open University Press
Buckingham · Philadelphia

For Meryl, Eileen, Alice and Max

Open University Press
Celtic Court
22 Ballmoor
Buckingham
MK18 1XW

email: enquiries@openup.co.uk
world wide web: www.openup.co.uk

and
325 Chestnut Street
Philadelphia, PA 19106, USA

First published 2001

A catalogue record of this book is available from the British Library

ISBN 0 335 20240 3 (pb)   0 335 20241 1 (hb)

Library of Congress Cataloging-in-Publication Data
Aldridge, Alan (Alan E.)
  Surveying the social world: principles and practice in survey research/
    Alan Aldridge and Ken Levine.
      p.   cm. — (Understanding social research)
    Includes bibliographical references and index.
    ISBN 0-335-20241-1 — ISBN 0-335-20240-3 (pbk.)
    1. Social surveys—Methodology.   2. Questionnaires.   I. Levine, Kenneth,
    1945–.   II. Title.   III. Series.

HM538.A53 2001
300′.723—dc21   00-068921

Typeset by Type Study, Scarborough
Printed in Great Britain by Biddles Limited, Guildford and Kings Lynn

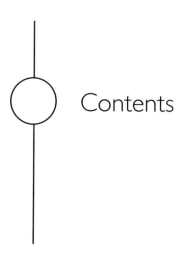

Contents

Series editor's foreword

This Understanding Social Research series is designed to help students to understand how social research is carried out and to appreciate a variety of issues in social research methodology. It is designed to address the needs of students taking degree programmes in areas such as sociology, social policy, psychology, communication studies, cultural studies, human geography, political science, criminology and organization studies and who are required to take modules in social research methods. It is also designed to meet the needs of students who need to carry out a research project as part of their degree requirements. Postgraduate research students and novice researchers will find the books equally helpful.

The series is concerned to help readers to 'understand' social research methods and issues. This will mean developing an appreciation of the pleasures and frustrations of social research, an understanding of how to implement certain techniques, and an awareness of key areas of debate. The relative emphasis on these different features will vary from book to book, but in each one the aim will be to see the method or issue from the position of a practising researcher and not simply to present a manual of 'how to' steps. In the process, the series will contain coverage of the major methods of social research and will address a variety of issues and debates. Each book in the series is written by a practising researcher who has experience of the techniques or debates that he or she is addressing. Authors are encouraged to draw on their own experiences and inside knowledge.

This new book on surveys by Alan Aldridge and Ken Levine is very much in tune with the aims of the series. It is concerned to bring out not just the principles that are involved in survey research but also a host of practical issues. However, in survey research there are different contexts to what might be meant by a term like 'practical issues'. Quite rightly, Aldridge and Levine refer quite often to large, frequently complex exercises in survey research to illustrate some of their main points. But for many, if not most, readers of this book such a context is very far from the reality they will be facing if they wish to carry out a social survey. It is this second scenario with which this book is largely concerned. Students, whether undergraduate or postgraduate, are likely to have limited resources and invariably limited time at their disposal. Texts on survey research that focus primarily on large, lavishly funded national surveys are hardly pertinent to such a situation. Aldridge and Levine's book is full of advice on how to devise survey research in the kind of environment that typically confronts a student: namely, having a fairly tightly focused set of research questions that are to be answered using a survey approach, but with limited resources.

Aldridge and Levine bring their experience of conducting a relatively small-scale survey on a highly focused topic – travel to work decisions and behaviour of staff and students at their university – to put some flesh on the bones of the principles of survey research. They bring out the kinds of issue that need to be taken into account when conducting such research. In the process, they identify crucial decisions about the conduct of surveys: what kind of sample to select, whether to interview or to use a self-completion questionnaire, how to design survey questions, and so on. In addition, they address various hardware and software issues and provide a helpful over-view of approaches to quantitative data analysis.

But it is the sense of being in on the reality of what it is like to do a survey that distinguishes this book from others on the survey approach and that will prove indispensable to future survey researchers. Social surveys are rarely if ever perfect. However, there are numerous traps that can ensnare the unwary and this book will alert readers to ways of avoiding them, as well as introducing the realities of survey research.

Alan Bryman

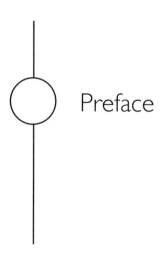

Preface

In an era in which 'social inclusion', 'active citizenship' and 'customer-centred' feature among the popular buzz words, it is not surprising that an increasing number of individuals and institutions are attracted to the social survey as a way of consulting interest groups, audiences and clients. Surveys abound, but many of the people who will carry them out lack any formal training in social research methods and need guidance about principles as well as practical know-how.

There is no shortage of existing textbooks that deal with social surveys and some of them have established worthy reputations. However, for the purposes of the non-professional people mentioned above and also for students being introduced systematically to the method for the first time, many existing works have one or both of two drawbacks. First, they fail to distinguish between the possibilities open to an individual or small group conducting a modest survey on a limited budget, and what is possible for a research centre commanding a sizeable team sustained on the basis of a sub-stantial research grant. A variety of strategies and techniques are ruled out if the resources and staff to implement them are lacking, and we have tried to signal throughout what is feasible in small-scale and solo projects. Second, some textbooks make the successful completion of a social survey appear extraordinarily unlikely. There is a tendency to counsel perfection and to appeal to ideals without practical workarounds being offered. There seem to be so many traps, hazards and obstacles that only an Indiana Jones, propelled by massive determination and superhuman powers of foresight, could overcome them all. While it is true that there are a variety of factors that have to be entertained, we set out to reassure readers that surveys can indeed be conducted by ordinary mortals. We have not neglected the problems and pitfalls but we have tried to offer alternatives and remedies wherever possible. Beyond that, we have sought to strike a positive note and to offer reassurance at the few points it is likely to be needed.

Part of the editorial brief we were given was to avoid a heavily statistical approach. The analysis of survey data, even for small-scale investigations, necessarily involves the selection and use of statistical tools, so this is not an easy task. We have concentrated on the general role played within surveys by descriptive and inferential statistics, seeking to maintain a focus on how they fit in with the other dimensions of survey analysis and referring readers to other sources for the step-by-step detail of procedures.

Both of the authors have been associated with the Survey Unit at the University of Nottingham, UK, and one of the investigations it conducted, the *Travel Survey*, is used as a running example throughout the book. We would like to take this opportunity to thank the present and past staff of the Unit, Jan Wagstaff, Beth Rogers, Nerys Anthony, Dr Nicola Hendey, Helen Foster and Becky Nunn for their hard work and good humour in innumerable projects. The undergraduates from the School of Sociology and Social Policy (formerly the School of Social Studies), together with postgraduates from various departments taking the Quantitative Methods module, also deserve our thanks. They have confirmed once again that teaching and learning are always two-way processes. We acknowledge the contribution of Sue Parker in the School of Sociology and Social Policy, an ever-helpful source of support and encouragement to student learning in modules involving surveys and statistics. Our thanks are due to Paddy Riley of Academic Computing Services, University of Nottingham, for the benefit over many years of his expertise with SPSS and other computer packages. Finally, we are indebted to Professor Alan Bryman, the series editor, for his many helpful suggestions. All of the above remain entirely blameless for any errors of omission or commission.

① Why survey?

Key elements in this chapter

- Our approach
- What is a social survey?
- Four methods of collecting data
- Three types of face-to-face interview
- Surveys, experiments and case studies compared
- Critique and defence of surveys
- Strategies to encourage respondents to take part
- Ethics of survey research

Our approach in this book

Every book on social surveys is trying to be helpful. Despite the good intentions, it is all too easy to be unrealistic and off-putting. Why is this? We suggest the following reasons:

- *Checklists of do's and don'ts*: The don'ts always seem to outnumber the do's. Survey research sounds like a minefield.
- *Counsels of perfection*: Any failure to abide by the do's and don'ts appears

to invalidate the whole survey. Many readers sense they will never match up to this ideal, so why bother trying?

- *Too much technique, not enough imagination*: The design and analysis of surveys involves technicalities – hence the do's and don'ts. But if that were *all* there is to it, it would be very dull. Luckily, it does not have to be like that. Successful surveys involve an exercise of the sociological imagination, as well as skilful use of techniques. Survey research is a craft, like throwing a pot, and brings much the same satisfactions (and frustrations).
- *Statistics*: Statistical analysis is a powerful instrument, and it is foolish to attack it. But statistics are tools, not an end in themselves. The hard part is usually not the statistics, but the sociological imagination.

If these are the problems with books on social surveys, how have we dealt with them?

Using and extended example

We use a recent and real life example of a survey, which we refer to throughout the book, to illustrate the practical and theoretical issues which arise at each stage. Thus throughout you will find discussions of the *Travel Survey*. The purpose is to examine the planning and execution of a single real survey that you can follow step by step to see how the different aspects and activities that make up a social survey fit together. Many chapters contain a box focusing on features of the *Travel Survey* relevant to the topics dealt with in that chapter. The *Travel Survey* questionnaires are reproduced in Appendix 1.

Box 1.1 The *Travel Survey*

The *Travel Survey* was commissioned from the Survey Unit at the University of Nottingham, UK, early in 1998 by the administrative department responsible for buildings, parking and transport facilities. They needed information on the commuting habits of students and staff, so that they could fulfil the commitments they had given to the local authority to minimize the traffic congestion likely to be caused by the construction of a new satellite campus about half a mile from the main site. They also wanted to preserve the parkland character of the main campus by encouraging 'environmentally friendly' forms of commuting such as buses and bicycling.

The survey was intended to generate detailed data on commuting patterns and related attitudes among staff and students that would enable transport consultants to advise the university on a variety of 'green' policies. Thus its objective was primarily *descriptive* rather than *analytic*: the task was to describe variations in commuting patterns rather than to offer explanations of them.

The sociological imagination

Like all methods of social research, surveys call for an exercise of the sociological imagination. In surveys, as in fieldwork, we have to 'take the role of the other' (George Herbert Mead's phrase); that is, we make an imaginative leap into the roles of our respondents, trying to get inside their experiences, their private troubles, their joys and aspirations, and their ways of thought and expression. We have to be sensitive to nuances of language, to the wider culture, and often to the organizational and occupational setting. We have to avoid stereotypes and stereotyped thinking.

Box 1.2   The sociological imagination: sensitive topics

In the 1960s, a team of sociologists at the University of Cambridge, UK conducted an investigation into the values, beliefs and social activities of relatively well paid working-class people: the *Affluent Worker* studies. As part of their survey, they asked a sample of respondents to keep a diary logging their weekly social and leisure activities. Some respondents were embarrassed that most of their leisure time was spent on everyday activities like mowing the lawn, cleaning the car and going shopping. They were worried that the researchers would think their lives were dull – an example of the **social desirability*** problem. This example reminds us to be imaginative about what the potentially sensitive topics are likely to be. Looking at it positively, sensitive issues also tend to be the most interesting sociologically and the most important socially.

Being realistic

Every researcher knows that compromises have to be made and desirable things left undone. We often have the simple choice: make the best of it, or do nothing.

Box 1.3   Being realistic: no time to do a pilot

In 1993, Aldridge was approached by a senior administrator at the University of Nottingham, UK. The university's Management Group was debating whether or not to build a day nursery on campus for the children of students and staff. They were not sure what the level and pattern of

---

* The first use of a term included in the glossary is printed in bold.

demand would be. Could Aldridge help by conducting a survey of staff and mature students?

This was half-way through October. The Vice-Chancellor wanted a report and recommendations by mid-December. After discussion, it was agreed that this could be put back to early January at the latest.

Strictly, Aldridge did not have the time and resources to do the survey 'properly', in textbook fashion. But it seemed a very important project. Better that the university have some objective information to go on than none at all. Aldridge therefore went ahead, but had to make some compromises. He decided that there was no time to conduct a **pilot survey** to test the question wording for all the problems that can arise. All surveys are supposed to be carefully piloted; to omit this is risky. (It is not, despite the impression sometimes given, unethical.) Aldridge decided to do the following:

- undertake crash reading about nursery provision, to identify the key issues (Aldridge knew very little about the topic);
- show the draft questionnaire to a few friends and colleagues, asking them to be extremely critical and pull no punches;
- keep the questionnaire as simple as possible, covering only the key issues and avoiding anything fancy;
- spend a lot of time on the **covering letter**, to try to ensure that the questionnaire would be well received by a very diverse group of respondents: not just academic staff and students, but secretaries, porters, cleaners, ground staff and so on; not just people with infant children, but childless people, childfree people, and people who would have been desperate for a nursery but for whom it was too late because their children were grown up;
- dispense with a follow-up (reminder) letter, even though it would certainly have boosted the response rate;
- keep the analysis straightforward and the final report short and to the point.

Happily, it turned out well. The **response rate** was reasonable, respondents were very cooperative, and the report was written on time. The Vice-Chancellor was pleased. *And* the university decided to build the nursery.

Our readers' experience and resources

We are writing mainly for readers who have had very little experience if any of doing a survey. Some readers will have taken part in a survey as a respondent – which may or may not have been a stimulating experience.

We are also assuming that, in most cases, the sort of survey the reader will be likely to undertake, at least to begin with, will be a relatively small-scale one with limited resources. These can be very worthwhile – size is not the most important thing. The reader may well be working solo or, if not, in a small team. The reader may be a student, or someone wanting do a survey on behalf of an organization. Although our book does sometimes refer to large-scale surveys like the General Household Survey or the Census, we are not primarily writing about those. After all, if you are working on such a survey you will receive training and be told what to do!

Hints and examples

Each survey is unique. Therefore, lists of do's and don'ts are too inflexible. A solution in one survey may not work in another. We provide general hints, not inflexible rules. We also give real examples of how we have tried to solve problems in our own research. We use our *Travel Survey* for the University of Nottingham as an extended example running throughout the book.

Statistics

Our aim is to introduce the broad principles of statistical analysis, to clarify *which* statistics are appropriate *when*, and to indicate what statistics can and cannot do. We provide suggestions for further reading on the technical aspects.

What *is* a survey?

A social survey is a type of research strategy. By this we mean that it involves an overall decision – a strategic decision – about the way to set about gathering and analysing data.

The strategy involved in a survey is that *we collect the same information about all the cases in a sample*. Usually, the cases are individual people, and among other things we ask all of them the same questions. This is the type of survey we concentrate on in this book.

The items of information we gather from our respondents are the **variables**. Variables can be classified into three broad types, depending on the type of information they provide:

- *attributes* – that is, characteristics such as age, sex, marital status, previous education
- *behaviour* – questions such as what? when? how often? (if at all)
- *opinions, beliefs, preferences, attitudes* – questions on these four characteristics are probing the respondent's point of view.

We shall examine the nature of variables more fully in Chapter 2. For the moment, the key point is that a survey aims to gather standard information in respect of the same variables for everyone in the sample.

Methods of data collection in surveys

Social surveys employ a variety of methods to gather information, such as questionnaires, face-to-face interviews, telephone interviews and observation.

Questionnaires

These are forms containing sets of questions which the respondent completes and returns to the researcher. One main type is the **postal (/mail) questionnaire**, which is sent and returned through the post. Questionnaires may also be completed and returned on the spot, for example in a classroom or dentist's waiting-room. The rapid growth of email has opened up another interesting possibility for the distribution and return of questionnaires.

Face-to-face interviews

In this book we do not refer to questionnaires when talking about interviews. Rather, we say that the interviewer has an **interview schedule** (for use in a **structured interview**) or an **interview guide** (for use in an **unstructured** or **semi-structured interview**). (Some sociologists use 'questionnaire' more broadly, to include interview schedules. When they want to make the distinction, they use the term **self-completion questionnaire**.)

Face-to-face interviews can be classified into three types: structured, unstructured, and semi-structured.

1 In a structured interview, the questions and the question order are pre-set. The interviewer aims to be in control of the interaction, and the respondent is just that – someone who responds to questions that are put to him or her. The interview schedule is like a questionnaire, except it is read out and filled in by the interviewer.
2 In unstructured interviews, neither the questions nor the question order are predetermined. Unstructured interviews are exploratory, and in principle non-directive: it is more like a focused conversation. The aim is to enable people to express themselves in their own words, highlighting their own feelings, preferences and priorities rather than those of the researcher. Although there is no interview schedule the interviewer may well have an interview guide, consisting of a set of prompts to remind them what main topics need to be covered.
3 A semi-structured interview is one which aims to have the best of both worlds. Parts of the interview are structured, with a set of questions directed in sequence to the respondent, while other parts of the interview are relatively unstructured explorations of particular or general issues.

Unstructured interviews are widely used in therapy and counselling. They clearly do not meet the requirement, intrinsic to the survey method, that standardized information is gathered systematically from all respondents. A survey, by definition, cannot be wholly based on unstructured interviews. This does not mean that survey researchers and non-directive interviewers have to be at loggerheads. Throughout this book we point to the advantages of multi-method research strategies. Questionnaires, unstructured interviews, focus groups, participant observation, diaries: all these methods, and others besides, can be combined in imaginative and innovative ways.

Telephone interviews

The nature of telephone interactions with strangers implies that telephone interviews are invariably of the structured variety.

Observation

Examples of surveys based on observation are traffic censuses, and studies of pedestrian flows through city centres (very useful commercially to anyone wanting to know where to set up shop).

Surveys and other research strategies

The survey is one of the three broad research strategies available in social research. The others are the **experiment** and the **case study**.

The experiment

Within the social sciences, experiments have tended to be conducted almost exclusively by psychologists. Some experiments are carried out in the laboratory, others in natural settings, 'in the field' – though it is far harder for field experiments in the social sciences to match the ideal type of the so-called 'true' experimental design. Amid the wide variety of types of experimental design we can distinguish the following key features.

Experiments are usually designed to test *hypotheses* (tentative explanations and predictions) about the *causal relations* between variables. The researcher carefully controls the **independent variables** (the potential causes) in order to measure their impact on the **dependent variables**, the effects. The people taking part in the experiment, the subjects, are divided into two or more groups, on the basis of a **random assignment** of individuals to groups. These groups are exposed to different experimental treatments. Statistical tests are used to determine the extent to which any differences in the measurement of outcomes (dependent variables) are due to each independent variable.

In an experiment, the researcher deliberately introduces a difference between the people taking part. For example, take a clinical trial in which some subjects receive a new drug designed to relieve headaches, while others receive no treatment at all. Very often, no treatment means being given a **placebo** – a harmless preparation which has no medical value or pharmacological effects. At the outset, each subject stands an equal chance of being in the experimental group receiving the drug or in a **control group** receiving no treatment or the placebo.

Clearly, it would be hopeless if all the men were put into one group and all the women into the other, because then we would not know whether differences in outcome were due to the drug or to the sex of the participant. Random assignment of individuals to groups is a statistically derived technique for addressing the problem that other independent variables, in this example the subject's sex, might be causing the differences in the dependent variables, in this example headache relief.

Equally clearly, it would be no good if subjects knew whether they were receiving a drug or a placebo. If they did know, it might well affect their response to the treatment, thereby invalidating the experiment. For this reason, *active* placebos are sometimes used – that is, placebos which mimic the side-effects of the drug but without its hypothesized therapeutic benefits. Very often, it is also desirable that the researchers themselves do not know, at the time they are administering a treatment, whether it is a drug or a placebo. If they did know, they might unintentionally communicate their feelings and expectations to their subjects, subtly implying that the drug would work whereas the placebo would not. An experiment or clinical trial in which neither the subjects nor the researchers know, during the experiment, to which group the subjects have been assigned, is known as a *double blind* procedure.

In surveys, by contrast, the researcher is dealing with differences between respondents that are given, not experimentally created. Men and women, smokers, people who have given up smoking and people who have never smoked, car drivers, motorcyclists, cyclists and pedestrians: we do not experimentally create these differences, our respondents present them to us.

The case study

As the name implies, a case study involves an in-depth investigation into a particular example of a social phenomenon or institution. Two areas of sociology in which case studies have played a prominent part are the sociology of education, where detailed work has focused on social interactions in classrooms, staffrooms, playgrounds and so on, and the sociology of religion, where studies have focused on minority religious movements such as the Moonies (Barker 1984), examining, for example, the relationship between Moon and his followers, and probing the question, have members exercised choice or are they brainwashed?

Case studies typically involve a wide range of research techniques, including observation, **participant observation**, interviews, documentary analysis, and asking people to keep a diary. They may also involve some survey work – case studies and surveys are not incompatible.

The success of the survey

Modern survey research is the fruit of a long and complex history of social, scientific and philosophical development. We tend to take surveys for granted, but viewed historically they are an achievement. Survey research today is underpinned by discoveries in sampling theory, multivariate analysis and scaling methods. Readily obtainable computer packages make sophisticated analytical tools widely available. Fundamental ideas such as the concept of the *respondent* – a person who is both the object of enquiry and an informant – were very slow to develop (Marsh 1982: 19). These advances took place in a range of disciplines – sociology, psychology, demography, geography, marketing, organization research, statistics – and this contributed to their success, since no one discipline had a monopoly on the survey.

In First World countries, surveys are found everywhere, and are conducted by all manner of organizations, both large and small, from government agencies through large business corporations to small voluntary organizations. If surveys were as hopeless as some of their more extreme critics suggest, it is hard to explain why they are so widespread and so enduring. Box 1.4 gives an example of a survey whose impact has been incalculable.

Box 1.4 Smoking and lung cancer

In the first half of the twentieth century, lung cancer death rates increased sharply in several countries. By the 1950s, there was evidence from both laboratory work and studies of hospital patient records that appeared to implicate smoking as a factor. However, the tobacco companies and some doctors remained unconvinced, arguing that atmospheric pollution and improved diagnosis were plausible alternatives and that the causal processes underlying respiratory cancers had not been identified.

In 1951, Richard Doll and A. Bradford Hill (with the later collaboration of Richard Peto) embarked on a major **epidemiological** study of smoking and cancer. They arranged for the British Medical Association (BMA) to send questionnaires about smoking behaviour to every doctor on the *Medical Register* in Britain at four points over the next 21 years (eliciting responses from over 34,000 individuals). They also traced and analysed the death certificates of 10,072 doctors who died over the period.

The results (see, for example, Doll and Hill 1952 and Doll and Peto 1976) showed that the lung cancer death rate of those doctors under 70 years who smoked was twice that of lifelong non-smokers of comparable age, with increased death rates for other respiratory tract conditions and degenerative heart disease.

Although the research did not attempt to explain what it was about smoking that caused lung cancer and the other associated conditions, it did provide large-scale evidence of a link between smoking and ill health. This evidence was hard to refute and impossible to ignore. The report's publication marked a significant turning point in official and public awareness of the dangers of tobacco smoking. Some other noteworthy features of the study are listed below.

- Doctors were selected not because of any especially high or low levels of smoking or any suspected special susceptibility to cancer, but mainly because they were a population likely to be interested in the research, motivated to cooperate and capable of reporting their smoking accurately and honestly.
- Another reason for choosing doctors was the existence of an accurate and ready-made **sampling frame**, the *Medical Register*, which meant there would be less difficulty in tracing doctors than a sample from the general population.
- The study was able to show that the risks of death increased steadily with the number of cigarettes smoked.
- It also revealed significant reductions in the death rate of the group of doctors who gave up smoking compared to those who continued to smoke. The overall death rate from lung cancer declined over the course of the study as many doctors gave up smoking, while other non-respiratory cancer rates remained stable.
- The consistency of the lung cancer death rate among doctors across different areas cast doubt on both atmospheric pollution and diagnostic improvement as major contributory factors. If these two had been operating, a differential between rural and urban rates would have been detected.
- The study put the onus on those sceptical of the smoking–cancer link to find a factor that varied *simultaneously* with the incidence of smoking (the **independent variable**) and disease rates (the **dependent variables**).

Among the most potentially important but also problematic surveys are those which involve international comparisons. One example is discussed in Box 1.5.

Box 1.5   An international survey of adult literacy

Comparative survey research may seek the collection of data from respondents who belong to different ethnic groups, cultures or nation states. The design of such studies requires both methodological and administrative problems to be addressed. Without sacrificing a standardized approach, the data collection instruments may need to be translated into different languages and to use quite different forms of expression to reflect divergent cultural perspectives. Practical considerations can rule out the use of self-completion questionnaires (rural postal services may be inadequate). The idea that certain low status social categories (children, unmarried women) will give their opinions freely to strangers in private interviews may be locally unfamiliar or unacceptable.

The International Adult Literacy Survey, conducted on behalf of the Organization for Economic Cooperation and Development in 1994, was an attempt to establish the comparative levels of adult literacy and numeracy in eight developed societies (Canada, Germany, the Netherlands, Poland, Sweden, Switzerland, the United States and Eire) using a suite of common tests and schedules (OECD 1995). A research team from each nation conducted a probability sample that was designed to be representative of its non-institutionalized population aged 16–65. In total, well over 20,000 individuals were involved. In Canada, respondents were given a choice of English or French test materials; in Switzerland, the sample was restricted to French-speaking and German-speaking cantons with respondents required to use the corresponding language. Respondents completed a test booklet and their demographic and employment details were gathered in an interview lasting, on average, one hour, conducted in their homes. People with very low levels of literacy were screened out of the samples by initial test questions.

Among the general findings were marked national differences: for example Sweden had large proportions at the top levels of the numeracy and literacy scales with small proportions at the lowest level, while the position in Poland was the reverse. There were also strong links in all countries between being currently unemployed and low levels of literacy. However, the significance and implications of the findings of such complex surveys is open to challenge. The measurement procedures used rest on assumptions that can be contested while the nature of the causal links lying behind the observed differences, in this case links between individual skills, employment and economic development, may be contentious. For a critique of the IALS, see Levine (1999).

Critiques of surveys

Over the years there have been numerous criticisms of social surveys as a research strategy. We can classify them into two broad, diametrically opposed types: scientific critiques and humanistic critiques.

Scientific critiques of surveys

Critiques of this kind are often mounted by people for whom the experimental method is the only valid means of arriving at scientific findings. According to them, surveys may display some of the trappings of science – reliance on statistical analysis, use of jargon, the appearance of objectivity – but all this is superficial.

The charge is that surveys cannot be scientific because the variables are not properly controlled. In experiments, the researcher makes strenuous efforts to control for the possible effects of extraneous independent variables. In a randomized clinical test, for example, everything is geared to measuring the effects of the drug. That and that alone is what interests us. Experiments are designed to isolate a very small number of key variables so as to measure the causal relations between them.

Surveys, in contrast, are sprawling constructions, typically involving a large number of variables covering a respondent's attributes, behaviour and opinions. No valid causal inferences can be drawn from survey research, it is said. If we find a **correlation** between, say, respondents' religious affiliation and their level of educational attainment, we have no way of knowing what the causal mechanisms are or even, in many cases, in which direction the causality runs. The most that can be hoped for from a survey is some descriptive material that may suggest hypotheses which can be scientifically tested through an experimental design.

Humanistic critiques of surveys

In this perspective, the problem with surveys is not that they fail to be scientific, but that the aim to be scientific is misconceived. This critique has a number of dimensions.

One major objection is that surveys are *atomistic*: they treat society and culture as no more than the sum of the individuals within it. The sociology of religion provides an example. Can we really measure the religiosity of a society by asking a sample of the population about their own religious beliefs and behaviour? Arguably, we should assess the social and cultural importance of religion by examining the influence of religion on the education system, on the law, on the political process, and on the commercial decisions of business corporations (Aldridge 2000). If our investigation shows that religion has little influence, then society has been secularized –

religion has lost social significance – even if our surveys show that the majority of people say they believe in God.

Paradoxically, although surveys are atomistic they are not really concerned with individuals at all. The thrust is to produce aggregate data: 80 per cent are this, 55 per cent think that, 2 per cent do the other. The language of survey research betrays its lack of concern with the individual: respondents, samples, cases. And what are statistics, if not a means of analysing aggregate data? Focus on the individual human being, and the statistician is silent.

One strand in the humanistic critique of survey research has been trenchantly expressed by Blumer (1956) in his attack on the limitations of 'variable analysis' – by which he means the reduction of social processes to the correlation between variables. These variables, he argues, are not generic: they do not stand for abstract categories, and so cannot be generalized beyond the specific context of the survey. They are locked into what Blumer calls the 'here and now', which, we may note, soon becomes the 'there and then'. The depressing conclusion is that variable analysis results in knowledge which is neither generalizable nor cumulative. Nor does it offer any insight into the interpretive processes through which social reality is constructed.

According to the humanistic critique, surveys are only marginally less artificial than experiments. Surveys cannot overcome the problem of the **reactivity of research instruments**, because they are by their very nature a crashing intrusion into the normal flow of social life. Respondents are self-consciously behaving as respondents. One obvious and ineradicable expression of this is the problem of social desirability. Respondents' answers are influenced by their desire to be helpful and to live up to their own self-image or to an ideal which they think will look good to the researcher. Respondents will therefore over-report their virtuous acts and play down or ignore their failings and foibles. They will also try to appear consistent, with the result that their opinions and beliefs will seem more coherent than they really are.

Part of the artificiality of surveys, according to critics, is that they are driven by the concerns of the researcher rather than the respondent. The essence of a social survey is to put questions to respondents. Whatever efforts we make to allow respondents to express themselves in their own words, we cannot go very far. It is simply not possible in a survey design to have a large number of **open-ended questions**, where respondents are free to answer in whatever words they choose. Most of our questionnaire or interview will inevitably consist of **closed questions**, where we present a series of choices from which respondents are asked to choose.

It follows from this, say the critics, that we shall find it almost impossible to gauge the **salience** of issues to our respondents. It is we, after all, who are raising the issues in the first place. We can of course ask respondents how important given issues are for them. Even so, this is hardly a solution to the social desirability problem. Admitting to a researcher that you have no interest in issues apparently deemed to be important is a difficult thing to do.

Some critics conclude from all this that the only valid use of surveys is to gather basic factual information, as in national censuses. Market researchers can use surveys to find out what products we buy and what possessions we own. This, however, is hardly the stuff of a vibrant social science. It is mundane, untheorized fact-grubbing – what C. Wright Mills (1970) called *abstracted empiricism*. It shows, what is more, that the basic function of social surveys is to provide useful information to people who have power over us. Some draw the devastating conclusion that surveys are an instrument used by Orwellian Big Brothers to keep tabs on the proles.

Response to the critiques of surveys

Few sociologists nowadays see sociology as a hard science on a par with nuclear physics or microbiology. Most people agree. For that reason, the scientific critique of surveys is less pressing than the humanistic critique. Despite the scientific critique, we believe that surveys have a part to play in establishing causal relations, as we shall explain. But causality is always complex because society is complex. Decades of research into the effects of the mass media, including a host of true experiments, have produced very little hard evidence. The truth is – though pressure groups find it impossible to accept – we simply do not know much about the effects of the mass media, and perhaps we never will.

For us, for our students, and we suspect for most of our readers, it is the humanistic critique that is potentially the more damaging. Our response to it, developed throughout the book, is in essence, this.

Poor surveys

It is sadly true that too many surveys are poorly designed, badly executed and incorrectly analysed. They yield nothing of value. Clearly, though, exactly the same is true of ill-conceived experiments and botched field work. 'Rubbish in, rubbish out' applies to all research strategies. Our aim is to promote the cause of good surveys.

A multi-method approach

Surveys can be fruitfully combined, in all sorts of imaginative ways, with unstructured interviews, observational fieldwork, documentary analysis, focus groups and so on. Using more than one research strategy enables us to **triangulate** data, that is, to use a variety of methods to test the **validity** and **reliability** of our findings. We give examples in Chapter 3. We do not accept that surveys cannot address sensitive and subtle issues. In our view, it is disastrous to erect a sectarian barrier between surveys and fieldwork, quantitative and qualitative methods. As Oakley has argued (1998), one danger is the creation of a gendered hierarchy of knowledge in which quantitative research is represented as objective, hard-edged and masculine, while qualitative research is subjective, sensitive and feminine. The apparently sharp opposition between quantitative and qualitative research is a social construct that perpetuates patriarchy; upon serious examination, all social research turns out to have quantitative and qualitative elements.

The role of social theory

Social surveys can play a significant part in the development and testing of sociological theory. Surveys do not have to be fact-grubbing. It is worth adding that in many cases so little is known about a topic that a few facts would not go amiss.

Servants of power

It is true that survey research is useful to commercial organizations and to the state. On the other hand, survey research can give a voice to the general public, to consumers, and to disadvantaged and disprivileged groups. This brings us to the social context of surveys.

The social context of surveys

Social surveys as we understand them are a modern phenomenon. They developed during the period of industrialization, and came to full fruition in the twentieth century. The British Census began in 1801, and has been carried out every ten years since that date with the exception of 1941, at the height of the Second World War. Similarly, the decennial (ten yearly) Census of Population in the United States began in 1790. Two of the most important surveys ever carried out in the UK were Charles Booth's *Life and Labour of the People in London* (published 1889–1902 in seventeen volumes) and Seebohm Rowntree's study of York, *Poverty: A Study of Town Life* (1902). A number of influential surveys were carried out by *Mass Observation*, which was founded in 1936 and which had a keen sense of a mission to inform the general public about the state of the nation. In our own times, major national surveys include the *General Household Survey* and the *Labour Force Survey*. In addition to these large-scale affairs, there are countless small surveys taking place every week of the year (though they slacken off during major holidays). There is every sign that surveys will continue to flourish in the twenty-first century and beyond.

Social surveys are also a feature of First World societies. They depend upon strong central institutions and advanced communications infrastructures. The Third World cannot always afford them, and the command economies of the communist societies had less need of them. At the time of writing, the former communist countries are experiencing profound conflicts in their transition to a market economy, a liberal-democratic polity and a consumer society. Their problems are not just economic but social and cultural. The neglect of serious survey work was characteristic of their lack of responsiveness to consumer interests.

Reading texts on social survey design and analysis written in the 1960s and 1970s can be revealing. At times it seems almost another world. The social scientist typically comes across as an authority demanding cooperation from respondents. A cultural gulf lies between us and them. These respondents are incompetent. They will misunderstand our interview questions and mess up our questionnaires unless we give precise instructions and spell everything out in minute detail. Similarly, the survey director, a man, will have to give lengthy training and detailed instructions to his hired-hand interviewers, who are women. These women, like the respondents, tend to get things wrong unless their work is closely monitored. The alienated labour of the mass production assembly-line is thus reflected in the closely controlled routines of the hired-hand researcher. The advice given in these texts is not so much poor as out of date.

The language of this era carries over into contemporary research, and much of it can feel uncomfortable. The people who take part in our research are conventionally called 'respondents', which may suggest a stimulus–response model of our relationship with them. Some researchers think it would be better to speak of 'informants', as the social anthropologists do, to acknowledge the point that people are supplying us with information which they have and we want. At least, unlike many psychologists and medical researchers, we do not refer to people as 'subjects'.

Another unfortunate word is 'instructions'. When we ask people to fill out questionnaires, we need to give them guidance on what we are looking for, as well as some explanation of the rationale underlying our questions. This guidance is conventionally termed 'instructions', even though we do not have the power of command that the term appears to imply. People can refuse to be interviewed, or put the phone down on us, or throw our questionnaire into the waste paper basket. They can also complain to us, our sponsors or our employers, as we have both discovered.

In some ways, this language of 'respondents' and 'instructions' does not matter. After all, we do not use it in talking *to* the people we are surveying; it is an occupational discourse we employ among ourselves to talk *about* them. The point is, we need constantly to remind ourselves about our relationship with our respondents. Just as a commercial firm which treats its customers as 'punters' is likely to lose business, so a survey which sees respondents as ignorant dimwits is a survey scarcely worth doing.

Today, more than ever before, people are uneasy about the way in which social surveys use aggregate data. In surveys we are typically comparing men with women, smokers with non-smokers, and car drivers with cyclists and pedestrians. Individuals are submerged into a category – which we may find objectionable. People have complained for years about sociologists' alleged obsession with social class. In the words of Number 6, the lead character in the 1960s cult TV series *The Prisoner*: 'I am not a number, I am a human being!' The more we can persuade our respondents that their own *individual* experience and opinions count for something, the better.

Reflecting on the socio-cultural context of surveys can help us to identify the reasons why people are willing to take part in them and the main sticking-points. From these reflections, we can draw some broad conclusions about basic principles which can guide us in designing our research.

Why are people willing to take part in surveys?

Helping the researcher

This has always been one of the most powerful motives for filling out questionnaires and agreeing to be interviewed. People want to be helpful. Unfortunately, their help may take the form of telling us what they think we want to hear. This is another example of the social desirability problem, one of the main challenges that confront the social researcher.

Altruism

As well as helping the researcher, respondents are often motivated by the hope that the research will promote social progress. People volunteer for all sorts of social activities in order to make the world a better place. Richard Titmuss's classic work (1970), *The Gift Relationship*, uses the UK's voluntary blood donor system as a case study of the power of altruism.

Citizenship

Responding to surveys can be a way of expressing one's democratic right as a citizen to have a voice in public affairs. This is probably the main reason why people turn out to vote in elections. Even if our vote is unlikely to make any difference to the outcome, we may still hold it important to have our say in the democratic process. So it is with surveys. This implies that people's motivation to take part in a survey will be strengthened if they believe that their expressions of opinion will count for something.

Let's talk about us

Often, we survey not the general public but a particular group within it: students, clergy, people with literacy problems, members of an ethnic minority and so on. In such surveys it is normally clear to respondents that the reason they have been selected is that they are *members* of a particular group or stratum in society. Our survey gives them the chance to be *representatives* of their group. Taking part in survey research is one way a group of people can gain a hearing for their opinions, experiences and ideas. This motive can be very powerful when a group feels a sense of grievance that its point of view has been misunderstood and its problems ignored. Luckily for us, most groups feel that way.

Let's talk about me

Given appropriate safeguards, people like talking about themselves. It may not always be the noblest motive, but if we expect our respondents to be saints we should consider an alternative career to survey research.

In the next section, we discuss some of the reasons why people may be reluctant or unwilling to take part in surveys. Very often, motives are mixed. People may have strong reasons both to participate and not to do so. Box 1.6 gives one instance of this ambivalence.

Box 1.6   Establishing the 'dark figure' of unrecorded crimes

In the late 1960s, the US government sought to expand its intelligence about crime and criminals beyond the information available in the *Uniform Crime Reports (UCR)*, the standard format in which official police and court statistics are presented in the USA (of similar status to the Home Office's *Criminal Statistics* in the UK). One objective was to estimate the size of the *dark figure*, the volume of crimes that had actually been committed but which, for various reasons, went unrecorded in the UCR. Researchers adopted an ambitious design which included surveys of selected US cities and of businesses in order to gather information on levels of white collar crimes like fraud. However, the most influential strand was a survey of the general public, based on eliciting details from a representative sample of US households about the occasions on which household members had been the victims of eight major types of crime, defined in the same way as they were in the UCR (Coleman and Moynihan 1996: 71–2).

The first US nationwide victimization survey in 1972 suggested crime rates three to five times those of the UCR. Despite a variety of methodological problems, including doubts about the accuracy of respondent recall and the capacity of the researchers to translate the respondents' common sense definitions of offences into the legalistic framework of the UCR, the findings commanded considerable public and official attention.

Although the use of victimization surveys spread quickly beyond the USA, the British government waited until 1981 before commissioning the first national UK survey which was conducted in 1983. Over time, the methodology used has been refined and the research objectives expanded to cover the processes underlying the non-reporting of incidents and the variety of roles victims can play in precipitating crimes. Victimization surveys are now generally accepted as an important complement to orthodox criminal and judicial statistics, though the initial claim that they could establish the 'true' prevalence of crime is now regarded sceptically.

Self-report surveys, in which samples of the population are asked about their own offending, are a further way in which the orthodox official statistics can be supplemented. Inviting respondents to admit they have broken the law, or even that they have engaged in lesser kinds of deviant conduct, necessitates very careful question design and interviewing technique. Self-report surveys have been used extensively in connection with so-called victimless crimes like drug abuse, and also with schoolchildren regarding smoking, substance abuse and under-age alcohol consumption.

Why are people reluctant to take part in surveys?

Decline of deference

It used to be said popularly that Britain was a class-conscious society, riven by class distinction and snobbery. In sociological terms, what was being referred to was not class but *status*: looking up to or down on people depending on their social background, occupation, education and style of life compared to your own. Profound social and cultural changes are eroding these status-conscious patterns of thought and behaviour, as demonstrated by the *Affluent Worker* studies of the 1960s (Goldthorpe *et al.*). One consequence is that social researchers can no longer expect deferential cooperation from 'ordinary' people. What is true of Britain is true elsewhere.

Scepticism about experts

Linked to the decline of deference is a growing scepticism about the expertise of scientists and professionals. Highly publicized scandals have reduced public confidence in the pronouncements of experts. The BSE crisis in the UK is one dramatic example. One practical consequence is that simply mentioning a university or scientific affiliation in a covering letter is no longer accepted as a guarantee of honourable intentions in the way it once was.

Consumerism

The rise of consumer society is one of the key issues in contemporary sociology. Consumerism implies choice, including the choice of *exit* – in this case, refusal to take part. It may also imply an orientation towards cost–benefit analysis: why should I take part? What will I gain, and what will it cost me in time, effort, or frustration?

Competition from market research and salespeople

Social scientists are not the only people conducting surveys. The fact that commercial market research relies on surveys as a principal source of information is a sign of the power of the survey method. Salespeople sometimes pretend that they are conducting a survey when they are really trying to sell us something (a tribute vice pays to virtue). Telephone sales pitches routinely begin with the false assurance, 'Don't worry, Mr Aldridge, I'm not trying to sell you anything'. We need to distinguish our own research from these other activities.

Survey fatigue

Arguably, there are just too many surveys going on. People get fed up (technically, **survey fatigue**), and are not willing to take part in yet another survey unless it is well designed and seems especially worthwhile.

Intensification of social life

The society of leisure, once predicted in the 1960s, has not yet arrived. Many people feel under increasing pressure at work. All sorts of therapies are available to help people cope with the stress of modern living. Our telephone call, our ring on the doorbell, our questionnaire on the doormat, may seem like yet another intrusion into people's precious free time. Our surveys need to come across as part of the solution, not part of the problem.

Dislike of form-filling

One source of stress is filling out official forms. We have yet to meet anyone who enjoys doing their tax return. A questionnaire which feels like an official form is probably not one that will achieve a high response rate. So, too, an interview that is experienced as an interrogation is unlikely to yield rich information or deep insights.

Privacy

The concept of 'the information society' has received a lot of attention from sociologists (Webster 1995). People are concerned about the data that commercial and public agencies hold on them; hence many societies have passed laws on data protection and freedom of information. In general, people are nowadays far more suspicious about the uses to which data are put than they were in the past. This means that any guarantee of **confidentiality** has to be seen to be watertight. If the researcher can guarantee **anonymity**, so much the better, even though it can raise problems for the researcher. The nature of the guarantee of confidentiality or anonymity should be realistic and crystal clear.

Box 1.7 Encouraging people to take part in surveys: general lessons

- *Value of the research*
  We presumably think that our work will be valuable. The more we can convince respondents that this is true, the better. Wherever possible, we should find ways of feeding the main findings back to our respondents and to people like them.
- *Value of respondent's contribution*
  Why should a respondent bother to answer our questions, when they have plenty of other things to do? What difference will their participation make to the value of our research? Some respondents are worried that they have nothing original and interesting to say, or that they don't know much about the topic. We need to convince people that their own individual response is important.
- *Being explicit*
  In modern societies, respondents are increasingly sophisticated and critical. They are familiar with surveys, and alert to deceptive techniques of persuasion. Many people are concerned about the researchers' hidden agenda, their sources of funding, and the uses to which the findings will be put. We need to make the rationale of our research as explicit as possible.
- *A humanistic approach*
  Many respondents, and most sociologists, do not believe that sociology is a hard science like nuclear physics or inorganic chemistry. If our style of research – for example, rigidly structured questionnaires and interviews, with little opportunity for respondents to express their own views in their own words – suggests that we are treating people as the objects of scientific research, we are likely to encounter resistance. People should have the opportunity to express their views in their own words.

Research ethics

Professional research ethics can be seen in the context of the wider cultural factors we have just been reviewing. The fundamental principles of research ethics flow from the nature of the social relationship between researcher and respondent, a relationship which is necessarily embedded in a set of cultural values, norms and codes of conduct.

All of the major professional bodies such as the British Sociological Association (BSA), the British Psychological Society (BPS) and the American Sociological Association publish guidelines on research ethics to which their members are expected to adhere. Appendix 2 suggests a few web addresses where these may be viewed.

The general principles of research ethics impact somewhat differently, depending on the research strategy chosen. Despite its different applications, the core of research ethics is due respect for the integrity of people participating in our research.

Respect for our respondents can be broken down into three key components: informed consent, confidentiality and sensitivity.

Informed consent

Compared to fieldwork observations, one potential virtue of surveys is that they are relatively overt. The problems of **covert research** are far less pressing for the survey researcher than they may be for the ethnographer working in the field. Even so, as survey researchers we need to be as open as we reasonably can be about the purposes of our research, the sources of funding, and the potential audiences for and uses of our findings. We should make it easy for respondents to raise any queries they may have. In some cases it may be desirable to give the name of a responsible person whom they can contact if they want to verify who we are and the nature of our research. In interviews, we should have proof of our identity readily available. It may also be desirable to indicate that our research has the approval or support of a relevant person or body – a trade union, say, or a charity. We also need to consider ways in which we can make a summary of our findings available to our respondents, so that informed consent comes to fruition in an informed outcome.

Confidentiality

Respondents are usually offered an assurance of confidentiality. In some cases this extends further to anonymity, which is the stronger guarantee that not even the researchers will be able to identify who the respondent is –

something which is only easily achieved in the case of self-completion questionnaires. Our assurances need to be as clear as possible, so that people are not misled. We also need to be aware that, in some cases, it is all too possible for a knowledgeable reader to identify a respondent even if we have given them a pseudonym and apparently concealed their identity. This is a particular problem when the researcher is surveying the members of an organization: there may be very few women or members of ethnic minorities, particularly in senior positions. How are we going to represent their responses while concealing their identity from their fellow workers and their bosses?

Sensitivity

One important area in which sensitivity needs to be exercised is in the use of language, particularly as regards 'race' and ethnicity, sex and gender, age, and disability. Examples of good practice can be found in other people's published work. A particularly useful source is The Question Bank, a resource centre funded by the ESRC (Economic and Social Research Council) and run by the National Centre for Social Research, and the Universities of Southampton and Surrey in the UK. Its internet address is: http://www.natcen.ac.uk/cass/. Language evolves, and varies cross-culturally in the English-speaking world, so it is important to keep up to date on acceptable usage in the culture in question.

While encouraging respondents to take part in a survey is entirely appropriate, attempting to put pressure on them is not. As citizens they have the right to refuse (except when there is a legal requirement to respond, as in the decennial Census). The potential for undue pressure is greatest in an organizational context, where people may feel that they will be judged 'uncooperative' if they decline to participate.

An invitation to survey research

Our book is an invitation to survey research. The word invitation implies joining in something worthwhile and enjoyable. Surveys can be both, we believe. There are, of course, problems and frustrations, and we have tried to be open about them. At the same time, we are positive. The problems are there to be overcome, and a successful survey can contribute to understanding social life in the hope of making things better.

Key summary points

- Surveys are a form of research strategy.
- They involve the sociological imagination.
- They have to capture the imagination of the respondents.
- They can be combined with other research strategies.

Points for reflection

- Does the word 'survey' make your heart sink? If so, why?
- If you had unlimited resources and a year to do it, would it be worthwhile to do a survey on behalf of your favourite charity, or would it be a waste of time?
- If you did that survey, how would you encourage people to take part?

Further reading

Marsh (1982) *The Survey Method: The Contribution of Surveys to Sociological Explanation* is an excellent account of the survey as a research strategy. It examines the major critiques and vigorously defends surveys against them. For a comprehensive account of the survey method see Babbie (2001) *The Practice of Social Research*.

2 Theory into practice

Key elements in this chapter

- The components of the modern social survey
- The characteristic features of the survey as a research strategy
- Types of survey design
- Relationships between theory and research
- Integrating theory in survey research
- Indicators and tests
- Validity and reliability

The components of the modern social survey

In Chapter 1, the social survey was defined as a strategy in which the same information was collected from all the cases in a sample (or for the whole population of interest). This definition now requires some elaboration. Because it is broad, it covers a great many of the exercises conducted throughout history by agents of ruling elites in order to establish, for example, the population numbers of key ethnic, religious or occupational groups, the scale of enterprises for tax collection purposes, or the manpower available for military service. In this book, however, we are primarily concerned with the survey in its contemporary forms. The modern survey is a synthesis of certain ideas and methodological innovations that were available to be used together only by the middle of the twentieth century. These components are discussed below and a partial explanation is offered to a question that may have arisen in the mind of some readers – why is the systematic social survey such a recent development?

Respondent/informant orientation

As suggested in Chapter 1, the idea that the provider of the information in a survey is a respondent or an informant is an important conceptual development, in itself reflecting changing ideas of citizenship and social participation. Informants deserve to be treated with respect as knowledgeable and, within limits, reliable, their cooperation has to be carefully sought and their rights acknowledged (for example, to have the information they provide treated confidentially). There are exceptions to the definition of respondent offered in Chapter 1: some are proxies for the real subjects of the inquiry (parents for small children, members for the organizational teams of which they are part); some censuses and other official surveys do impose legal sanctions for non-cooperation. Nevertheless, the modern survey revolves around identifying strategic informants, persuading them to cooperate, and painstakingly constructing questionnaires and interview schedules containing questions that will be meaningful to them. Information collection is the principal aim with other objectives set aside or made subsidiary (these might include promoting awareness of goods and services or recruiting potential followers to a cause or interest group). In contrast, premodern surveys were often exercises in compulsion conducted on groups unable to refuse. In some cases, such as British nineteenth-century research on the poor, direct contact with the group itself was often minimized and the principal resort was to testimony from various expert intermediaries such as inspectors, the police or employers. The aims of such exercises were often very blurred and concern for the interests of participants was rarely paramount.

Standardized data collection instruments

The questions posed in pre-modern surveys were often ad hoc and ill-considered, unselfcritically reflecting the social worlds, assumptions and language of the authors (or the bureaucracies in which they worked) rather than the informants. There were additional obstacles to be overcome. Long after the inauguration of nation-wide mail deliveries, the use of postal questionnaires with samples of the general public was hampered by low levels of mass literacy and by widespread suspicion that the information being requested was an extension of surveillance by agencies of social control. Structured questionnaires and interview schedules with standardized wording and explicit definitions, wherever possible tested in pilot exercises on small groups of respondents, could only become an integral part of the modern social survey when the social infrastructure facilitated their use. A significant part of the effort in designing contemporary instruments is devoted to making the resulting schedule or questionnaire comprehensive, applicable to every respondent or situation that might be encountered. At the same time, user-friendliness is a major consideration: respondents need to feel at ease during interviews, while response rates for self-completion questionnaires are promoted if the forms are made as straightforward as possible by clear layout and helpful graphics.

Systematic selection procedures

The presumption that scientific thoroughness obliged social researchers to collect information from every member of a community or every household in the parish was an enduring one and probably delayed the social science application of the statistical ideas underpinning probability (random) sampling which were in circulation since the middle of the nineteenth century. The practical application of sampling theory to social surveys took place in the first decades of the twentieth century and the five towns inquiry by Bowley and Burnett-Hurst, published in 1915, was possibly the first British sociological study to include estimates of the reliability of findings based on samples (Marsh 1982: 26). Among other things, the advent of sample surveys solved the problem of having to secure the resources to fund large teams to process massive amounts of information from large numbers of respondents. This had previously locked surveying into fields where charitable or state support was forthcoming: sampling procedures helped to open the door for small groups and individuals to use the survey as a tool.

Multivariate analysis

The final core component of the modern survey and the most recent to be integrated with the others is multivariate analysis; that is, statistical procedures for analysing the relations between sets of variables whose values are varying simultaneously. Adequate descriptive statistics dealing with numerical observations have long been available. However, a key task in surveys with explanatory goals is to unravel causal processes after they have operated in the real worlds of respondents and the cultures and social structures in which they are located. Multivariate techniques can introduce statistical controls that eliminate complicating variables and enable answers to 'what if?' questions to be formulated. These techniques are crucial for unravelling complex issues where many factors are in play – how different social classes pass on differential advantages to their offspring over generations, the precise extent to which academic achievement is the product of home background, individual ability and school characteristics.

The widespread use of multivariate statistics for the analysis of survey data only developed after the Second World War. One of the factors that arrested its diffusion was the time and drudgery taken up by the elaborate statistical calculations involved. The advent of first mainframe then later desktop computers running software applications specifically designed for social surveys represented major advances. Investigators now possess an unprecedented capacity to explore survey data thoroughly using exploratory and analytic statistical tools.

Listing these four components may present an idealized picture of the modern social survey. Not every instance employs systematic sampling, while the objectives in some contemporary descriptive surveys render multivariate analysis superfluous. The point, however, is that the components are available for use in those research situations able to exploit them, and their joint use creates a tool of social inquiry of exceptional potential. However, effective synthesis does not take place by itself. Each component has a slightly different logic and requirements all of which require harmonization. The task in designing surveys is to make these four components fit together as seamlessly as possible.

The survey as a research strategy

This section considers some of the main characteristics of the survey as a research strategy, taking account both of its strengths and its limitations. As well as offering guidance on the choice between strategies, this discussion aims to help the reader assess how a survey could be linked to and coordinated with other types of research strategy so as to circumvent the limitations of each.

Extensive/intensive

Surveys are the prime example of an *extensive* research technique in the social sciences, one capable of gathering comparable information from respondents across a wide range of different social groups. One frequently-used tactic is to employ a survey in the first phase of a project to establish what the general outlines of the researchable problem are and then to use the data collected to design a more intensive second phase using case studies or other *intensive* approaches. For example, a hypothetical investigation into home working might use a survey to map the sectors of business and industry in which it was most prevalent and to establish what types of employee were working from home with what general levels of success and satisfaction. A second stage could then adopt a narrower but more detailed focus. On the basis of the results of phase one, it would probably be possible to locate organizations that use home-working intensively and also some that have tried and abandoned it, and to gather more information about the arrangements in these contrasting instances. Alternatively, it might be possible to set up a programme of in-depth interviews with individuals who have home working experience that would expand the data available on matters such as domestic management problems and communication with work colleagues.

This is merely an illustration of one major strength of the survey: it is also entirely possible, provided the topic and setting are suited, to design a survey that is aimed at a relatively small group of respondents and which collects detailed data from them in a single collection operation.

Naturalness/artificiality/intrusiveness

Surveys stand in an intermediate position between a highly naturalistic strategy such as participant observation and the clearly artificial laboratory experiment. A well-conducted interview has some of the character and familiarity of a normal conversation (and it may take place in the respondent's home, workplace or other familiar setting) but it is nevertheless a conversation with an interviewer who is normally a stranger. Although there are advantages speaking to respondents on their home 'ground', interviewers are usually entering an environment that has, to a greater or lesser extent, been prepared to receive them, so the situation cannot be regarded as entirely authentic. Indeed, if there is limited space and privacy, an entirely 'normal' and authentic situation can undermine the possibility of conducting any kind of interview because of interruptions from other family members, colleagues or the telephone.

Street interviewing is self-evidently highly intrusive and refusals are common. Self-completion instruments such as email or postal questionnaires are low on naturalism but they have the balancing advantage of allowing the respondent to select the time for their completion, an option that significantly reduces their intrusiveness.

Qualitative/quantitative

Surveys are often characterized as a pre-eminently quantitative research strategy but this is a misperception. A prime advantage of surveys is precisely that they allow the simultaneous collection of both types of data. Open-ended questions are not simply devices to deal with the cases not covered by the closed categories offered in a previous question. The material they elicit can open up important insights into respondent motivation and perceptions. There are, of course, limits on the extent to which the respondents to postal questionnaires can be expected to write lengthy essays on their views or preferences, and these are situations in which personal inter-views may be preferable. In general, the capacity of surveys to deliver mutu-ally supporting qualitative and quantitative data should not be neglected.

Causal inference

In some textbooks, the social survey is compared unfavourably with the experiment and is portrayed as a poor and logically deficient relation. As noted on page 8, this is largely because the classical laboratory experimenter has the advantage of being able to manipulate the key independent variables in 'real time'. In addition, confounding factors can be controlled through the laboratory isolation of the subjects and their random allocation to the experimental and control groups. In terms of making causal inferences from data, the laboratory experiment appears to have a major advantage over the survey which, as we have seen, has to reconstruct naturally-occurring causal processes after they have taken place (*ex post facto*) through statistical manipulation of the data. One of the several problems this creates is ambi-guity about the precise sequence of changes and thus potential uncertainty over whether the data implies causation or only co-variation. There are two points to be made here. The first is that a properly designed survey should be able to reconstruct causal relationships, but it requires careful design and it necessitates a sample large enough to permit the use of sufficiently sophisticated statistical tools. Second, the analysis above neglects the role of theory: without an adequate theoretical framework in play, neither the experimenter nor the surveyor is in a position to identify which are the salient variables to include in the design or to make appropriate inferences about any patterns in the observed data.

Flexibility/rigidity

A frequently overlooked difference between research strategies is the differ-ent degrees of flexibility they permit the researcher. Some essentially quali-tative research strategies allow a preliminary analysis of the first wave of data so that the outcome can be used to determine the venues and the topics to be pursued in the second wave, and so on. This alternation between data collection and analysis is especially useful in preliminary research where there are many parallel avenues that could be explored, in the light of which the researcher wants as many options left open as possible. Surveys do not lend themselves to such a rolling strategy. They may be thought of as 'front-loaded' in the sense that a series of major interlocking decisions covering all the main components mentioned under the previous key heading need to be made before any data collection can begin. Once testing and piloting have been completed, the standardizing logic of surveys prohibits changes to the definition of the target population, the sample design or the contents of the questionnaire/schedule. It is not possible to change tack if early responses do not live up to expectations. This rigidity reinforces the emphasis that should be placed on thorough preparation and pre-testing.

Types of survey design

There are three basic designs for surveys that reflect the main directions of comparison that will be made at the data analysis stage.

Cross-classificatory (cross-sectional)

In some senses, this is the fundamental survey design. There is a single stage of data collection (sometime referred to as 'single shot') and the unit of analysis is a case with all of its characteristics (variables). Although a case is frequently equivalent to a respondent, this is not inevitable (the case might actually be a household and the respondent simply a member providing information about its expenditure patterns or leisure activities). The main focus is the comparison of aggregate groups of cases characterized by different values on key variables rather than the profile of characteristics possessed by any particular case. The objective is to see if groups of cases have co-varying values on other, dependent, variables. The *Travel Survey* is an example of a cross-sectional survey. The aim is to see what characteristics go with the choice of different modes of travel for the journey to work and what attitudes are associated with, for example, car use as against the use of bicycles or public transport. The analysis of stand-alone cross-classificatory surveys revolves around the construction and comparison of such sub-groups. Part of this design's strength lies in the way an analyst can chop up a sample into many quite different sub-groups to explore the separate dimensions of the research topic.

Longitudinal and panel studies

In a longitudinal survey, data collection takes place repeatedly in order to monitor the operation of social processes over time (the data generated are known as **time series**). In the special case of a panel study, the same respondents are involved at each stage (allowing for drop-outs). The British Household Panel Survey (see Box 2.1) is a large-scale example of a panel study. The presence of time as an explicit dimension in these research designs makes certain kinds of causal inference much easier. There are various statistical techniques tailored to the requirements of longitudinal studies: these include those based on ARIMA (AutoRegressive Integrated Moving Average, also known as Box-Jenkins models) and actuarial techniques dealing with the differential survival of cases in a population.

Hierarchical

In this more complex design, the main line of comparison is between the characteristics of a case and the characteristics of a collectivity in which the case is a unit or member. One of the principal research aims in hierarchical designs is to trace the influence of the collectivity on its members. An illustration of the application of hierarchical analysis would be a study of the recidivism – relapsing into crime – of the ex-inmates of a prison. The research question might be whether recidivism was closely connected to the characteristics of the prison such as its physical location, staff characteristics and the average length of sentences, and whether any of these factors interacted with features of the personal biography of the individual inmates (such as the number and type of offences they had previously committed) so as to increase the chances of further offending. Notice that there are two logically different kinds of variable involved in this design: prisons have some properties as institutions that cannot be inferred from the aggregation of the characteristics of individual inmates (and vice versa). Multilevel statistical models are available to facilitate the analysis of this kind of two-level data.

As well as showing that the nominated independent variables co-vary with the nominated dependent variables, all three types of design must include the capacity to detect the operation of rival independent variables that could lead to misinterpretation of the findings. The identity of these rival variables may be self-evident, or alternatively the main candidates will have been proposed in the research literature. One example of a potentially confounding variable is differential exposure to atmospheric pollutants as an alternative cause of cancer in the study discussed in Box 1.4. This factor was controlled in this study by the ability of the investigators to demonstrate that there was a higher cancer prevalence for smoking doctors than non-smoking doctors across both rural and urban locations, where atmospheric pollutants would be absent and present respectively. A further example is the need to control for individual ability while studying the impact of class size and teaching styles on pupil academic achievement (see Bennett et al. 1976). Confounding variables need to be measured and statistically controlled, or alternatively be excluded entirely from a design (for example, by defining the target population narrowly).

Relations between theory and research

The natural way to launch this topic is to define 'theory', but this must be done in a preliminary fashion so as to avoid discussions that would go beyond the scope of this book.

- There is a wide measure of agreement throughout the social and natural sciences that theories are the most important and the most intellectually

Box 2.1   Panel studies

Some of the largest scale surveys use a panel design. One of the most important in the UK is the British Household Panel Survey (BHPS) administered by the Institute of Social and Economic Research at the University of Essex. In surveys of this type, a designated group of households are monitored over periods as long as a decade with repeated waves of data collection. This enables their response to general shifts that have occurred in the economic and social environment to be examined. Such research also provides insights into the manner in which the impact of *macro* factors (for instance, changes in the labour market opportunities for women) depends on *micro* factors such as the age and generational composition of a household.

Some studies attempt to interview all the adult members in the household, while others use a key informant to supply information on behalf of themselves and the others. It is common for a core set of basic questions to be used with every household, complemented by a selection from additional sets put only to households of a particular type (low income, single parent, gross income above a threshold). In some studies, the second generation households set up by the children from first generation families are tracked and incorporated into the research as they are formed. Such activities require large teams and substantial budgets.

For further information on the BHPS, see http://www.iser.essex.ac.uk/bhps/doc/index.htm

rigorous means of producing explanations of phenomena (and the most satisfactory basis for predictions). Observations that lack a theoretical underpinning cannot provide a basis for explanation or prediction.

- There is no consensus on what the precise technical specifications for a theory should be and only partial agreement over what constitutes an adequate explanation.
- Every systematic discipline possesses a changing set of concepts that organizes knowledge within that field and identifies the entities in the world with which inquiry is concerned. At least some of these concepts have an abstract and idealized character – their existence cannot be directly substantiated but must be inferred from their effects on what is observable. Some social science examples, more or less at random, include *perfect competition,* the *self,* the *Schumpeterian workfare state, governmentality.*
- There is an on-going debate between two main philosophical camps over the status of theoretical entities: realists believe they represent mechanisms and processes that do exist in the world, instrumentalists see them as

simplifying devices, helpful to make sense of research data but not to be credited with an independent existence (Chalmers 1999).

- A theory is a linguistic construction that, critically among a range of functions, states the existence of a general law-like relationship between two or more abstract concepts. Theories are frequently developed discursively by their authors so that the presentation is mixed up with extraneous illustration, comment and criticism: a *schematic* reconstruction of a theory strips it down to the essential propositions and it is these propositions that could be incorporated into a research design or might be invoked to interpret research findings.

- The orthodox perspective on explanation (the covering-law model) portrays it as having the form of a deductive argument, that is, one in which the truth of the premises guarantees the truth of the conclusion. The phenomenon to be explained is described within a statement that forms the conclusion of the argument: at least one of the premises has to be a statement formulating a law-like generalization borrowed from a theory (for example, 'revolutions occur during periods of rising mass expectations', 'suicide rates are positively associated with the degree of individualism in society'). The other premise states a list of 'initial conditions' or limiting states of affairs that have to be satisfied for the theoretical generalization to hold.

- All empirical research rests on some theoretical assumptions about what entities exist and are capable of being investigated. In some cases, the assumptions are made explicit and the perspectives acknowledged, in others they are implicit and need to be teased out. For example, even a thoroughly descriptive inquiry like the *Travel Survey* rests on a variety of theoretical premises. By asking about home addresses, number of cars in the household and work patterns, the assumption is being made that the selection of a mode of commuting is an essentially rational choice based largely on individual assessments of time, cost and convenience. However, choice of mode of transport could arguably rest on quite different and less calculative considerations. A preference for car use might reflect, at least in part, a desire for privacy and the feelings of invulnerability that some individuals associate with motoring. For others, car use is likely to carry strongly negative connotations because it is perceived as environmentally destructive. By omitting questions that could tap these considerations, the *Travel Survey* is effectively incorporating one theoretical perspective in preference to others. In summary, some kind of theoretical thinking is always an *input* to any empirical research.

- At the same time, research may have a theoretical *output*. The analysis of survey data, as Chapter 8 will argue, is never simply a matter of identifying statistically significant associations. The substantive and theoretical significance of such associations has to be established in the light of the theoretical perspectives built into the research design, or those available beyond it in the discipline or disciplines parenting the research.

- Textbooks on research methods tend to highlight the special and quite rare instances in which a research project revolves around the testing of specific theoretical hypotheses. It is more realistic, however, to acknowledge that a great deal of empirical research is eclectic, drawing on whatever bodies of theoretical thinking seem relevant. Rather than setting out to test a theory, most survey research is either exploratory or developmental in that it seeks tentatively to establish, or modestly advance, theoretical thinking on some topic. Such advance can be achieved in a variety of ways: one is by elaborating key concepts so as to allow a more refined application of a crudely articulated theory: another is to develop the measurement apparatus associated with an existing theory and thereby extend its scope into new areas of application. It is true that a great deal of research has exclusively descriptive goals, though even here secondary analysis can draw out explanatory possibilities unrecognized by the original investigators.

Incorporating a theoretical dimension into surveys

In the light of the discussion in the previous section, it should be apparent that creating a survey that incorporates theoretical thinking is an exercise that demands some creative thought. However, a checklist always helps!

1 Will the designated target population have the appropriate attributes for exploring or testing the theoretical perspective(s) of interest? (see Chapter 4, page 63)
2 Will the chosen survey design permit the relevant logical comparisons to be made that exploring or testing the theories requires? Will the temporal order of changes in the values of variables be clear? (see the previous section)
3 Will the questions posed enable the derivation of all the variables that are central to a theory? Will the key theoretical concepts be adequately **operationalized**?
4 Even though they probably do not belong to the theoretical perspectives on which a survey is based, will there be data available on potentially confounding variables? (see the previous section)

Most of the items on this checklist are dealt with elsewhere in the book so the rest of this section concentrates on the issues raised in point 3 about how to operationalize theoretical concepts within surveys. The task is to find adequate indicators and measurable effects for theoretical mechanisms and processes which are not themselves directly observable or measurable. A leading American innovator in social science research methods, Paul Lazarsfeld, developed a strategy for breaking general theoretical constructs down into their measurable dimensions that has been influential (Lazarsfeld 1958), but this is a challenging task even for the experienced investigator.

There are three main types of measuring device that are used regularly in social surveys: derived measures; ready-made indicators; and psychometric, educational and other tests and scales.

Derived measures

These are simple indicators devised by investigators themselves and built from the responses to a series of questions posed in the interview or questionnaire. A derived variable will usually be constructed in the first stages of data analysis by some form of mathematical summation from several other variables contained in the codebook (see Chapter 7, pages 128–9). Demographic characteristics such as age, sex and family and household size are exceptional in that relatively few other variables of theoretical consequence lend themselves to measurement via the responses to a single direct question. Box 2.2 provides an example of derived variables used in the *Travel Survey*.

Ready-made indicators

There is a vast range of social, economic, health, educational, social psychological and other types of indicator that have been used in social science research. Some have established positions as standard measures: although not necessarily flawless, their widespread use in the past guarantees further use in the future as new projects seek direct comparability with older ones. The following examples are chosen more or less at random:

- The proportion of pupils in a school eligible for free school dinners is widely used in Britain as a rough and ready comparative measure of the level of social deprivation in the school's catchment area.
- The proportion of households not owning a car, available from British Census data, is similarly used as a simple indicator of the socio-economic character of urban neighbourhoods.
- The Retail Prices Index (RPI) is a key measure of inflation in the UK economy as it affects consumers.
- Deaths per million passenger miles travelled is used in studies of accident risk that wish to compare different modes of transport (planes versus cars) or different environments (motorways versus other trunk roads).
- Box 2.3 examines the use of social class as an indicator.

Psychometric, educational and other tests and scales

There is a huge variety of pencil and paper tests dealing with personality characteristics, social attitudes, social psychological factors related to groups and team memberships, and other topics that could potentially be included in interview schedules or questionnaires. Selecting a single topic from the many possibilities, there are several measures of anxiety, depression and suicidal ideation available including the *Hospital Anxiety and Depression* questionnaire (HAD) (Zigmond and Snaith 1983) and the *Beck Anxiety Inventory* (Beck *et al.* 1988). The inclusion of such tests in research may pose a variety of difficulties. With the illustrations cited, there could be ethical problems in asking respondents whether they feel depressed or suicidal if there was any possibility that this could actually trigger such feelings. There are also practical considerations – will completing a lengthy test be boring or take up too much of the respondent's time? Will a fixed test procedure fit in with the rest of the interview or questionnaire? Finally, there are the issues of the adequacy of the measures themselves that are discussed in the next section.

Box 2.2   Derived variables in the *Travel Survey*

Respondents indicated a large variety of different combinations of main (question 3) and alternative (question 4) modes of commuting, partly because question 4 allowed multiple responses. There was a need to classify commuters into a small number of commuting groups for the analysis. This was done partly on the basis of whether and how the car (including motor bikes) featured in an individual's commuting pattern. Eight derived variables were created, each representing a mode of commuting that reflected a distinctive combination of responses to the two questions:

- Group 1 *Exclusive car users*: respondents who ticked one from boxes 5, 6, 7 and 8 in response to question 3 and also either 1 or any of 6, 7, 8 or 9 for question 4.
- Group 2 *Car users with some public transport*: ticked one from 5, 6, 7 and 8 for question 3 and also 3 and/or 4 from question 4.
- Group 3 *Exclusive users of foot or pedal bike*: ticked 1 or 2 for question 3 and also 1 or 2 and/or 3 for question 4.
- Group 4 *Exclusive users of public transport*: ticked 3 or 4 for question 3 and also 1 or 4 and/or 5 for question 4.
- Group 5 *Car users with some foot or pedal bike*: ticked one from 5, 6, 7 and 8 for question 3 and also 2 and/or 3 for question 4.
- Group 6 *Foot or pedal bike with some public transport*: ticked 1 or 2 for question 3 and also ticked 4 and/or 5 in question 4.
- Group 7 *Public transport with some foot or pedal bike*: ticked 3 or 4 for question 3 and also 2 and/or 3 for question 4.
- Group 8 *Foot or pedal bike with some car use*: ticked 1 or 2 for question 3 and also ticked any of 6, 7, 8 or 9 for question 4.

Only a handful of cases did not fit into any of these eight groups. No case could belong to more than one.

The resulting groups did reveal interesting associations with other variables including, fairly obviously, the availability of cars to a household (question 22). Although the *Travel Survey* did not gather respondents' views about the environment, this might be an additional direction in which associations could be found. This is a very simple example of how, generally, classifications based on derived variables can play a role in bridging the gap between the response to a specific question and constructs which are closer to the realm of theory.

Box 2.3   Measuring social class

Social class is a key concept in both classical and contemporary social theory. There is a voluminous debate, on the one hand over how the abstract conception should be formulated, and on the other about what empirical indicators are appropriate. Since 1911, the Registrar General's classification of what were originally called 'social grades', based on industrial group, occupation and level of skill, has been used in the United Kingdom as one of the principal empirical indicators of social class, particularly in officially-sponsored research (Rose and O'Reilly 1997: 1). This classification was originally devised by a medical statistician to examine differentials in mortality and fertility rates. It was renamed 'social class based on occupation' (SC) in 1990 by which point it had been used in innumerable research studies. The categories are as follows (OPCS 1991: 12)

I   Professional occupations
II   Managerial and technical (formerly 'Intermediate')
III Skilled occupations
     (N) Non-manual
     (M) Manual
IV   Partly-skilled occupations
V   Unskilled occupations

Over time, SC became increasingly incongruent with the prevailing theoretical approaches to social class and was also criticized for lacking reliability and validity (see page 39). A variety of alternatives, such as the twenty category classification by socio-economic group (SEG – OPCS 1991: 13–14), the Goldthorpe classification based on employment relations (Rose and O'Reilly 1997: 40–8), the Institute of Practitioners in Advertising's Social Grade Scheme (A, B, C1, etc), widely used in market research, and Erik Olin Wright's schema based on Marxian class theory (Wright 1985), have been devised and applied in empirical research.

In 1994, the Office of National Statistics (ONS), the UK government agency responsible for SC and SEG, commissioned a review of existing class classifications with the intention of producing a revised scheme. The 'collapsed', eight category, interim version of the revised socio-economic classification (SEC) which resulted, based largely on the Goldthorpe approach, is set out below:

1 Higher professionals/senior managers
2 Associate professionals/junior managers
3 Other administrative and clerical workers
4 Own account non-professional
5 Supervisors, technicians and related workers
6 Intermediate workers
7 Other workers
8 Never worked/other inactive

Unlike SC, SEC has been subjected to extensive testing to establish its validity using data collected by ONS from its Omnibus Survey and the Labour Force Survey. SEC also has much more explicit links with theory than the SC. A version was used in the 2001 Census in Britain.

In order to use the SEC in a survey, questions will be needed that elicit the following three characteristics from a respondent:

• occupation
• size of employing establishment (if any)
• employment status (employer, employee, self-employed, not active)

Reliability and validity

Using pre-developed indicators and tests gives prominence to the issues of reliability and validity. Reliability is a measure of the extent to which the results of an indicator or test are consistent over time. This consistency can itself be measured in the form of a statistical coefficient of reproducibility, often Cronbach's alpha, which is similar to a correlation coefficient (see page 152). There are several different comparisons that can be made to examine reliability:

• *Test–retest*: respondents complete the same instrument on different occasions.
• *Internal consistency*: if a psychometric or other pencil and paper test consists of many items tapping the same underlying concept, split-half methods can be used to compare the consistency of results between (say) odd and even numbered items.

- *Inter-observer reliability*: will different interviewers using the same schedule produce equivalent responses from the interviewee?

A rule of thumb often quoted is that reliability coefficients should be at least 0.7 though, as with many rules of thumb, it is precise but arbitrary.

Validity raises the question of whether a measuring device is actually connected adequately to the theoretical mechanism, process or construct it was intended to capture. Do, for example, high scores on the HAD questionnaire correlate with cases of clinically-definable depression? Once again there is a variety of approaches to justifying an instrument:

- *Content validity*: this is decided by a panel of experts who review whether a measure does everything it should: it is clearly a pretty flimsy test and raises 'who validates the validator' questions!
- *Concurrent validity*: this measures a construct's validity against an unimpeachable standard, another form of measurement which has itself demonstrable validity but which may be complex, expensive or have other restrictions on its use: such a standard is obviously not always available.
- *Predictive validity*: can the measure successfully identify outcomes and consequences? Do respondents scoring highly on HAD but without symptoms at the time of testing subsequently get diagnosed as clinically depressed? Because many factors may intervene after testing to prevent or delay outcomes, predictive validity is often hard to establish with certainty.
- *Construct validity*: this looks back at the performance of a measure over time, preferably covering a wide range of studies, to see if it has produced fruitful findings. Thus, it would be possible to review the use of (say) the SC measure of social class to see whether it was, and remains, an effective means of explaining health differentials, voting patterns and other phenomena which are theoretically linked to class membership. In fact, such a review of construct validity was conducted for the SC measure by an academic panel on behalf of the ONS. Their conclusion was that SC was not valid and recommended its replacement by SEC (see Box 2.3).

One of the significant advantages of using established measuring instruments is that the burden of establishing reliability and validity has already fallen on another's shoulders.

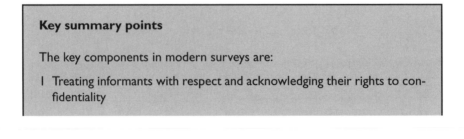

Key summary points

The key components in modern surveys are:

1 Treating informants with respect and acknowledging their rights to confidentiality

2 The use of standardized questionnaires and interview schedules designed with an emphasis on respondents' understanding and convenience
3 The use of systematic sampling techniques where appropriate
4 The use of multivariate statistical procedures in analytic surveys

A survey needs to establish:

1 The co-variation of key independent and dependent variables
2 The temporal sequence of changes
3 That no confounding variable could be causing the variation in the dependent variable(s).

For a survey to successfully explain or predict anything, it has to incorporate a theoretical dimension.

Points for reflection

- Is there a convenient review of the theoretical literature that you could use to justify and clarify your approach to the key research issues?
- Does your research design stand comparison with comparable projects? Does it address all the obvious confounding variables?
- Are all the key concepts adequately measured? If you have doubts, are there duplicate measures you can use?

Further reading

An excellent guide to the evolution of social surveys and also a defence of their utility, which is also referred to in the further reading for Chapter 1, is Marsh (1982) *The Survey Method*. The first three chapters of Hughes (1976) *Sociological Analysis: Methods of Discovery* are a good introduction to the connections between theory and research. Hughes and Sharrock (1997) *The Philosophy of Social Research*, 3rd edition, is a guide to different styles of research and the kind of philosophical underpinnings each has. There are several excellent introductions to the philosophy of science including Chalmers (1999) *What is This Thing Called Science?*, 3rd edition.

Miller's (1991) *Handbook of Research Design and Social Measurement*, 5th edition and Murphy *et al.* (1994) *Tests in Print* (IV) are among the guides to published tests and scales. Litwin (1995) *How to Measure Survey Reliability and Validity* provides a brief guide to the topic indicated by the title. (This latter volume is part of Fink, ed. (1995) *The Survey Handbook*, which contains small guides on most aspects of surveying.)

3 Planning your project

Reviewing your assets

In Chapter 2 (page 30), it was suggested that surveys were less flexible than some other research strategies because the need for standardization leaves little scope for modifications to be introduced in mid-course. Careful advanced planning is therefore essential. A realistic initial appraisal of the resources that you can bring to bear to carry out the survey will help to confirm that the operation envisaged is viable. It will also provide a basis for constructing an outline timetable that covers the whole of the project.

Background information and library resources

Even for small-scale community and in-house organizational surveys, preliminary research is desirable to confirm that the information being sought has not already been collected in other exercises. This will mean approaching personnel in the appropriate organizations and it will probably be necessary to reveal your intentions, at least in outline, in order to secure their cooperation.

Some library preparation is important for nearly all surveys:

- to establish what information is already available about the proposed target population;
- for surveys with an explicit theoretical dimension, to investigate how other research has applied the concepts and perspectives in which you are interested;
- to track down comparable previous research, especially previous surveys, even though they may have taken a different tack;
- to check any indicators or scales that you propose to employ.

Only the largest public libraries in major cities will be able to offer much help with some of these. Smaller public libraries in the UK should have *Social Trends*, an annual digest of official statistics published by the Office for National Statistics, and this is a very useful starting point in the search for statistical information published by and on behalf of government. The National Statistics website is at http://www.statistics.gov.uk/. For US information, the following are good starting points: http://www.whitehouse.gov/news/fsbr.html for links to statistical reports from US Federal agencies; http://www.gla.ac.uk/Library/Depts/MOPS/, a guide to the US Government statistics that are available on the Internet; http://www.fedstats.gov/ for links to over one hundred Federal agencies; http://www.census.gov/, US Bureau of the Census Site. For Australia, see http://www.abs.gov.au, Australian Bureau of Statistics information service. For Canada, see http://www.statcan.ca, Statistics Canada site.

Some of the background material will be in academic journals to which only university and research institute libraries subscribe. Inter-library loans can be arranged but they can be slow and a cover charge will be applied for each item. The findings and the instrumentation for many surveys are never published in an orthodox fashion for a variety of reasons: the documentation for them may have to be obtained by contacting the institutional sponsors of the research.

The University of Essex at Colchester, UK, has several resources of potential value to investigators planning surveys.

- The Data Archive is a collection of over 4000 datasets from surveys conducted in Britain and other countries, especially Europe and North America. These datasets are available to academic researchers as computer database files. The URL is: http://www.data-archive.ac.uk/
- Qualidata is the Economic and Social Science Research Council's archive of data from qualitative research projects which is itself searchable on-line. The URL is: http://www.essex.ac.uk/qualidata/
- The Institute for Social and Economic Research (ISER) is responsible for running several large scale surveys and much of the material related to them, including instrumentation and findings, is available on-line. The URL is: http://www.iser.essex.ac.uk/

Human resources

Even if you are conducting a survey in a solo capacity, there may be additional help you can call on for some of the labour-intensive tasks. Table 3.1 identifies suitable tasks that can be allocated to volunteers or casually-paid helpers. Some tasks like interviewing and coding should be given only to suitably trained and responsible assistants capable of working independently. Even an essentially routine task like preparing a mailshot can require supervision to deal with any complications. Some kinds of error that could occur at this early stage are not easily reversible and could jeopardize the entire survey. Always be cautious in your estimates of the productivity of inexperienced volunteers or paid helpers: they may face steep learning curves and they may not be as committed as you to quality and sustained performance.

Another kind of human resource is assistance from experts. Two kinds are mentioned later in the book. The first is the 'insider', a member or associate of the group that you are researching, or an employee within an organization in which you are carrying out data collection. Insiders can play an invaluable role particularly if no one in the research team has first-hand knowledge about the research groups or the venue. This kind of associate can help you before research begins with your request for access and your data collection instruments, and again after data collection with the interpretation and presentation of findings. The second kind of expert is a statistician, or anyone with substantial experience of research design and data handling, whom you may possibly need to consult regarding unusual or complex sample design and analysis problems.

One way to make the most of limited human resources is to buy in commercial research services for parts of a project. In principle, almost any element of the research process can be purchased from suitable agencies: in

Table 3.1 Delegable tasks in surveying

Task	Skills required
Checking databases, labels	Clerical, basic computer
Stuffing and unstuffing mailshots	Manual/clerical
Data entry	Basic computer
Telephone follow-ups	Basic communication skills
Transcription of taped interviews	Audio-typing

practice, costs are considerable and your budget, if it exists, may not stretch (although inquiries about approximate costs will do no harm). The most cost-effective element to sub-contract may well be data-entry: the key-boarders employed by specialized 'data capture' agencies can transfer all the responses from questionnaires or interviewer-completed schedules into a computer data file, offering the additional benefit of validated data entry (see Chapter 7). The charges are usually calculated from the total number of key depressions plus an initial 'set-up' fee. For instruments without a large number of open-ended responses, the costs can be very reasonable and the time-saving considerable.

Financial resources

Many people without experience of social research express shock and dismay when they are given a quotation for conducting what they consider to be a small-scale research project. There is an enduring belief that social research (unlike 'real' scientific research) can be conducted on a shoestring. Unfortunately, the fear that lay sponsors will baulk at the costs sometimes leads first-time researchers, anxious for support for a cherished project, to produce 'optimistic' estimates that underestimate the true costs and simply help to perpetuate belief in the shoestring. The list below gives some rough estimates of the costs, current at the time of publication, of selected elements of conducting a survey.

- It will cost at least £700 for an audio-typist to produce transcripts from twenty 45-minute taped personal interviews.
- Ignoring the design process, to distribute 2000 copies of a two-sided A4 postal questionnaire together with a one-sided A4 covering letter, and get back 1000 responses, allowing for photocopying, stationery, paying stuffers, and second class postage out and back, will cost around £1000.
- It will cost about £450 to have a data capture agency process the 1000 questionnaires, assuming there was an average of 250 key depressions per response.

Technical resources

Small-scale survey research fortunately rarely requires sophisticated equipment (beyond computers which are dealt with on page 47). One major exception is that projects based on tape-recorded interviews need to borrow or invest in a good quality audio-cassette recorder (preferably one with an auto-reverse on record facility so that the interviewer does not have to manually stop proceedings and turn the cassette over after 45 minutes). If a large number of interviews have to be transcribed, a dedicated cassette transcriber is preferable to an ordinary tape-recorder. These machines have a 'go back' facility that rewinds the tape a little and replays so that the typist can listen again to an inaudible phrase: they also come with a foot control and earphones.

Setting the timetable

Precise answers about how long any phase of a survey should take to conduct are difficult in the absence of hard information regarding the scale of the research and the resources available. Nevertheless, it is possible to provide some general pointers.

- You clearly need to work backwards from immovable deadlines (the delivery of the project report fixed by a sponsor, or a limited window of opportunity for data collection set by holidays or other restrictions on your access to the target population).
- It is usual to give respondents a minimum of two weeks to complete postal questionnaires.
- An extensive programme of personal interviews can be very time-consuming, especially if travel is involved: the overhead of arrangements (and re-arrangements) can be difficult to manage at the same time as actually conducting other interviews (can someone back at base do this?). Do not over-estimate the total number of interviews that a small team is capable of conducting, nor the time it will take to complete them.
- Transcribing tape-recorded interviews is also time-consuming: an experienced audio typist under optimum conditions might take four times the length of the interview for a full transcription of a personal interview. Focus groups are considerably more difficult because of multiple and overlapping speakers.
- Analysis expands to fill the time allotted for its completion: in most instances, it is best to settle on a finite period for the analysis in advance associated with a clear understanding of the minimum you hope to achieve within these limits.
- The overheads for collaborating can be considerable. Keeping each other

informed, getting people back on track after problems and a variety of other coordination tasks can eat into the productivity gains of having several hands. A team of three people rarely produces three times the output of one member.

Computing and software resources

Although it is possible to conduct a small-scale survey without computer assistance, it would be perverse to attempt it. Access to a desktop or laptop computer and suitable software is almost certainly the single most important resource that can aid the investigator in a survey project. A computer not only takes the drudgery out of numerical and textual data analysis but with suitable software it can help to design a professional looking questionnaire and ensure accurate data entry. Even a basic machine, equipped only with word processing and spreadsheet applications, can at the minimum help with project record keeping and correspondence. If there are suitable levels of computer literacy in play, such a machine can play a useful role in all phases of a survey.

Hardware

How ancient and limited a machine you can get by on depends very much on the scale of the project and the kind of software you envisage employing. Unless a machine has a hard disc and a central processor (CPU) of roughly equivalent power to an Intel 80486, it can probably be ruled out. (This is not meant to suggest that the computer must be a PC with an Intel or similar processor or running a version of Microsoft's Windows operating system.) The more sophisticated survey analysis packages tend to be demanding in terms of both processor power and memory requirements. Older machines with poorer specifications will certainly struggle to run them and may perform so slowly as to be unusable.

If there are several investigators and/or hired hands collaborating over a project, it is preferable to keep all the data files and other information in one location, invariably on a networked system, where access to them can be maximized. Equally important, there are grave dangers of generating unsynchronized and diverging versions of the same key files when different members of a team store their work in progress in different places.

Software

There are three main types to consider: standard business applications, one-stop applications, and dedicated applications.

Standard business applications

As implied above, a standard word processing application can be useful to create covering letters and to execute mailmerges for address labels. Self-completion questionnaires can be designed on word processors but it requires a little trial and error to get finely tuned results and there is rarely any help on how to get some of the unusual layouts that may be required. A standard office spreadsheet like Microsoft *Excel* is also extremely useful and can be used to store the data file (see Chapter 7) as well as to produce tables and charts. Although there are fewer ready-made solutions and less convenience than with a specialized survey package, it is nevertheless possible to carry out quite advanced data analysis and to produce excellent charts from a spreadsheet. Business databases such as Microsoft *Access* can also store the data file but they are often less intuitive to use and do not always have as extensive a range of graphical presentation facilities.

One-stop applications

A **one-stop application** offers a comprehensive and integrated suite of facilities for conducting surveys including questionnaire design, data entry, data analysis and presentation tables and graphics. There is clearly an advantage in terms of convenience in only having to cope with the interface for a single application, while there may also be cost savings to be had. At the same time, the statistical procedures available in one-stop packages tend to be more limited than those in the leading dedicated packages, though this may not be a problem for a small-scale project.

Examples of one-stop packages are:

- *PinPoint* and its successor *KeyPoint*, both published by Longman Software (the URL is http://www.longman.net/keypoint/). The latter incorporates facilities for conducting web surveys.
- *Sphinx Survey*, published by Sage Publications Software and distributed by Scolari (the URL is www. http://www.scolari.co.uk/). Some versions support the lexical analysis of open-ended responses.

Dedicated applications

A **dedicated application** concentrates on supporting a specific aspect of survey research, particularly data analysis. As a result, there tend to be more user options and a higher degree of sophistication than in a one-stop package. This can present problems for first time users who can get lost in a sea of difficult choices. On the other hand, there is a very good chance that exactly the facility you are seeking will be available 'off the shelf'. Dedicated software also exists for data entry and charting, but the choice in the data analysis field is especially extensive.

Examples of data analysis packages include:

- **SPSS** (Statistical Package for the Social Sciences), published by SPSS Inc (http://www.spss.com/). The grandfather of survey analysis software with a track record stretching back over 35 years, a very large international user base and associated with a wide range of linked products and services. Supported by extensive documentation and several textbooks (see further reading for Chapter 8).
- *GB Stat* (distributed by Scolari): offers good import facilities, graphing and export to word processors.

There are several general issues relevant to the selection of software packages for use in survey projects.

- Is it one-stop or dedicated? Can it deliver all the forms of analysis you expect to employ?
- Does it have good import and export facilities? In other words, can it recognize data files that have been constructed in other programmes and computer environments? If it lacks a particular facility, you may want to export some or all of the data to another package that does have it.
- Is the package well supported? This covers on-screen support, technical help-lines, web sites, and paper documentation. Does any of this help come at a price you cannot afford?
- Can it deal with the number of variables and all the types of data you expect to collect? In particular, if you have used open-ended questions, what facilities does it offer for processing the responses?
- Does it provide good presentation facilities (especially tables and charts) that can be imported directly into the word processor you are going to use to produce the report?
- Are there licence restrictions on the way it can be used which will conflict with the way you are planning to run the research? Is there an educational or charity price tariff?

Gaining access to organizations

In Chapter 5 (pages 86 and 90) we consider ways of approaching individual respondents and encouraging their participation. How we introduce and characterize our research on the telephone or in person, or in a covering letter accompanying a questionnaire, is crucial in securing participation and establishing rapport.

In many cases, however, our research is conducted in an organizational context. Our survey is not of the general public but of members of an organization, whether a commercial company, a union or professional association, a religious movement or a voluntary agency. In such cases the organization mediates our research relationship with our respondents.

On the face of it, the problem we face is this: gaining access to the organization so that we can survey its members. Whose authorization do we need, and what do we have to say and do to *get in*? This, though, is only one aspect of access. Access is not a one-off achievement but an ongoing process, with four dimensions (Buchanan *et al.* 1988): getting in, getting on, getting out and getting back. As Hornsby-Smith (1993) remarks, it can be helpful if we think of our involvement with the organization as an 'access career'.

Getting on points to the need to secure willing cooperation once we have been granted formal rights of access to respondents. Just because senior people have authorized our research does not necessarily mean that the rank-and-file will be enthusiastic. (When Aldridge arrived for one interview with a clergyman, he was immediately asked whether he was a spy from the bishop.) We need to win people over. In a complex organization we may well need to negotiate with a wide range of gatekeepers who can facilitate or hinder our research.

Getting out is also a sensitive process, despite the insensitive language. Getting out is not escape. Once we have gathered our data, we should not simply rush out of the organization breathing a sigh of relief. We have built up obligations to our respondents and to the people who have helped us carry the research forward. We will probably be feeding back our findings to them in one way or another, so we need to maintain our links to them.

One reason for handling getting out sensitively is the need we or others may have to *get back*. We may, for example, want to conduct follow-up interviews with key informants, or gather more information from company archives. The organization may itself ask us to carry out further work. Even if we have no intention of conducting further work in the organization, others may, so we owe it to them not to leave a sour atmosphere behind.

There cannot be a set formula for securing access in this fourfold meaning of the term. Patience and quiet persistence are often needed, as is the willingness to seize opportunities when they arise – they are seldom predictable.

Nor is it always easy to predict which organizations will be the most difficult to access for the purpose of conducting a survey, nor what barriers will need to be overcome. In virtually all cases, confidentiality will have to be negotiated carefully. The researchers may well need to demonstrate their competence to sceptics, since not everyone is convinced of the value of social surveys or the expertise of social scientists. Even when they are not sceptical, many organizations are so time-pressured that they need to be persuaded that their members can spare the time to participate. In some cases, ascribed qualities of the researcher such as gender, age, social status, ethnicity, religious affiliation can be a formidable and even impenetrable barrier. One advantage of using self-completion questionnaires (see Box 3.1) is their impersonality: the problem of interviewer effects does not arise.

Three methods of gathering data

We can distinguish three vehicles for gathering data from respondents:

1 *The self-completion questionnaire* In this method, respondents fill out the questionnaire themselves. It may be a postal (mail) questionnaire, which they complete and return by post. It may be a questionnaire handed to them, for example by a teacher in class or a receptionist in a waiting-room, which they are asked to complete on the spot and hand in. Or it may be an email questionnaire which they complete and return electronically.

2 *The face-to-face interview* Here the researcher interviews the respondent in person, either in the respondent's home, or in the researcher's office, or in some 'neutral' location. In social research, most interviews are one-to-one, though group interviews are also possible – interviewing the adult partners in a household, for example.

3 *The telephone interview* Here the interview is conducted over the telephone – or, in future, the videophone.

We set out in the boxes below the main advantages and disadvantages of each method, before considering the key choices to be made.

Box 3.1   Self-completion questionnaires: pros and cons

Advantages	*Disadvantages*
Cost The cost of reproducing and distributing questionnaires is relatively low.	**Questionnaire length** Self-completion questionnaires need to be short and also look short, or the response rate will be low.
Time to collect data Questionnaires can be distributed and returned quickly.	**Simple questions** Complex questions are cumbersome to ask and take too long to answer.
Large samples Because costs are low and data collection is fast, it is feasible to survey large samples of the population. The method benefits from economies of scale.	**Few open questions** Since written answers to open questions can take a long time, only a few such questions can be asked.

Geographical distribution
Since the researcher is not present, the sample can be drawn from a wide geographical area.

Response rate
Even with good design, response rates can be low unless respondents have strong reasons to participate. Response rates will be underestimated if questionnaires have been sent to people who are not part of the target population or who have moved address. Unless they let us know, we shall count them as refusals when they are not.

No interviewer bias
There is no interviewer to introduce unauthorized comments about the research, the questions or the respondent.

Control of context of response
The researcher often has no control over who fills out the questionnaire, nor the spirit in which they do so. Respondents can scan the whole questionnaire first, rather than follow the desired sequence of questions.

No interviewer effects
Respondents do not have to relate to characteristics of the researcher such as their age, sex, ethnicity, dress or accent.

Response bias
People who experience literacy problems, or whose mobility is restricted, will be less likely to respond.

Handling sensitive topics
Since the researcher is not present, respondents may find it easier to handle sensitive questions, particularly if their responses are anonymous.

Salience
Gauging the salience of items to the respondent can be difficult.

Box 3.2   Face-to face interviews: pros and cons

Advantages	*Disadvantages*
Length of interview schedule Because responses are verbal, it is possible to ask more questions that in a self-completion questionnaire. The appearance of the interview schedule is not relevant to the interviewee.	**Cost** Interviews are costly in money and time.
Complex questions The presence of the interviewer enables complex questions to be explained, if needed, to the interviewee.	**Sample size** Because of the time and money involved, one interviewer can conduct a limited number of interviews each day. There are no economies of scale.
Question skips As long as they are clear to the interviewer, question skips raise no problems for the respondent.	**Geographical restrictions** The cost of travel and the time it takes may limit the geographical reach of surveys carried out by interviews.
Open questions Since respondents do not have to write their answer, open questions can be used more freely.	**Time to collect data** Given that interviewing can be taxing for the interviewer, especially when interviews are not wholly structured, any one researcher can only undertake a few interviews each day – often four is the maximum.
Salience The use of open questions, and non-verbal cues for the respondent, enable the interviewer to gauge which items are salient to the respondent and which are of no concern.	**Interviewer bias** Interviewers can introduce bias by offering unauthorized comments on the questions, the research or the interviewee, which can lead the respondent in a particular direction.

Visual aids

Show cards can be used to help respondents frame their answer.

Ranking and rating questions

Relatively complex ranking and rating exercises are possible. For example, occupational titles can be written on cards, and respondents asked to rank them, or sort them into categories, based on criteria such as social status.

Control over context of response

In contrast to self-completion questionnaires, the researcher has control over who responds to questions and the sequence of questions. By establishing good rapport the researcher can ensure that questions are taken seriously.

Rapport

The interviewer's success in achieving a good relationship with the respondent will improve the quality of the answers.

Group interviews

Sometimes we would like responses from more than one person, for example, from the adult members of a household. This is only feasible in a face-to-face interview.

Interviewer effects

Personal characteristics of the interviewer – such as age, sex, ethnicity, dress or accent – can affect the way in which the interviewee responds.

Leading questions

Even without interviewer bias, leading questions can easily be introduced unwittingly into the less structured part of an interview.

Social desirability

The presence of the interviewer makes it even more likely that the respondent will seek to give socially desirable answers.

Anonymity

Although confidentiality can be guaranteed, anonymity clearly cannot.

Safety

Attention needs to be given to the physical safety of the interviewer, especially if interviews are conducted by one interviewer in the respondent's home.

Box 3.3   Telephone interviews: pros and cons

Advantages	*Disadvantages*

Cost
Costs are far lower than with face-to-face interviews.

Simple questions
Because strong rapport is hard to achieve, and because show cards are not possible, complex questions have to be avoided.

Large samples
Because costs are low and data collection is fast, it is more feasible to survey larger samples of the population than if interviews are face-to-face.

Response bias
Unless great care is taken, socially disadvantaged groups will be under-represented.

Geographical distribution
Since the researcher is not present, the sample can be drawn from a wide geographical area.

Sensitive questions
Telephone conversations are an unsuitable medium for asking sensitive questions.

Time to collect data
There is no travel time, and the respondent's agreement to participate is quickly obtained.

Open questions
Open questions are less effective than in face-to-face interviews. On the telephone, respondent's answers are usually brief, and probes have a limited effect.

Question skips
As in face-to-face interviews, provided they are clear to the interviewer question skips raise no problems for the respondent.

Limited response categories
Respondents cannot be expected to memorize a long list of response categories. Visual aids such as show cards cannot be used to help respondents frame their answer, as they can in face-to-face interviews.

Fewer interviewer effects
Although personal characteristics of the interviewer — such as age, sex, ethnicity, or social class — may be inferred, they are less obvious and intrusive than in face-to-face interviews.

Contamination by telesales
The telephone is widely used for selling goods and services, often with an initial pretence of conducting research. Genuine research is not always easily distinguished from these other activities.

Safety
The physical safety of the interviewer is not an issue.

Cold call
The telephone call comes 'out of the blue'; not having been prepared, respondents may be less likely to agree to take part.

Anonymity
Although confidentiality can be guaranteed, anonymity clearly cannot.

Self-completion questionnaires, face-to-face interviews and telephone interviews are the three main methods of gathering data in social surveys. We may add a fourth, as mentioned already in chapter one: observation. We should also note two variants on self-completion questionnaires: email and interactive surveys, and diaries.

Email and interactive surveys

These are electronic variants of the postal questionnaire, and they offer advantages along with some problems.

In an email survey, the questionnaire is distributed and returned electronically. This has advantages over paper questionnaires:

- we can pre-program the order of questions, so that respondents progress through the questionnaire in the sequence we desire without skipping ahead or going back;
- because of this, the problem of question skips does not arise – the program automatically moves to the next relevant question;
- the program can prompt respondents, and alert them to the fact that they have made a mistake – for example, if they try to tick several boxes where only one is required;
- there is no intermediate stage of inputting data; the data are available for immediate analysis;
- there are no problems about how to arrange for the questionnaires to be returned, and no intermediaries to intervene in the process of distribution and return;
- we can gain access through newsgroups to minorities who are hard to reach by other means.

There are, though, some major drawbacks:

- there is a sampling bias towards affluent, well educated, young, white, male citizens of First World countries – though this will become less acute as more people gain access to the internet;
- we need programming skills, or a programmer, to design the questionnaire;
- respondents need familiarity with and access to a computer equipped with the necessary software;
- respondents may lack confidence in the security of data sent over the internet and stored on a remote server or computer;
- anonymity cannot convincingly be guaranteed.

Diaries

Asking respondents to keep a daily record of their actions can be a useful part of a social survey. Potentially, it enables us to gather a large amount of data, much of which would be hard to obtain by other means. It can stand in for observation where observation is not possible.

We point out in Chapter 6 (see Box 6.6) that one of the most difficult problems facing the survey researcher is asking about periodic behaviour. Suppose we are interested in respondents' cinema-going. While a minority of them may have extremely regular behaviour – they go to the cinema every Saturday, as part of a regular night out – most respondents will not be like this. Their cinema attendance will be far more variable and hard to summarize.

One answer to the problem is to ask respondents to keep a diary of their activities day by day. We shall not have to depend on the respondents' fallible memory. Nor will we face the social desirability problem of respondents over-reporting socially approved behaviour and under-reporting socially stigmatized activities. A diary will provide us with a reliable record of their actual behaviour. Or will it?

Diaries are not a panacea for social desirability effects. Not only may respondents misreport their behaviour, *they may alter their behaviour* to conform with social norms. Keeping a diary makes people more self-conscious, and so may itself affect their actions.

It may be tempting to think of the diary as a low cost way of gathering data. The respondent does all the work and we reap the benefit. Of course it is not as simple as this. Diaries are difficult to design and to analyse. In survey research the diary is a form of self-completion questionnaire, one renewed every day. We should design it as such. Respondents need to know what to record and when to do so. As with questionnaires and interview schedules, we have to be selective, and as helpful as possible in explaining to the respondent what we are asking them to do and why. We need to be clear about the use to which the data will be put, including the issue of anonymity or confidentiality and any feedback we intend to give on the results of our analysis. We should contact the respondents in person or by telephone during the course of their record-keeping, to thank them for their participation, answer any queries, and encourage them to carry on. We should also, ideally, arrange to call to collect the diary in person. Diaries are, then, labour-intensive for the researcher too.

Sometimes, to keep the data manageable, the researcher asks only a sub-sample of respondents to keep a diary. One problem here is response bias: perhaps certain kinds of respondent will be more willing to do so than others.

Choosing a method of gathering data

In surveys conducted by a solo researcher or a small team, practical considerations often limit the options open to us.

If a large sample is required, or if respondents are geographically scattered, face-to-face interviews are normally impossible because they consume too much time and money.

If we need to ask a lot of questions, and if the format is complex, with multiple question skips, then a self-completion questionnaire is unsuitable, unless it can be distributed electronically. The more questions there are, the more a face-to-face interview becomes appropriate.

If we need to ask a lot of open questions, face-to-face interviews are to be preferred (see Boxes 3.1, 3.2 and 3.3).

Combining methods of data gathering

The methods of data-gathering we have been discussing are not mutually exclusive. It is often possible to combine them, with beneficial results.

Using a questionnaire to generate follow-up interviews

The rationale is that the questionnaire will provide basic information about the sample from which generalizations can be made to the whole population. Interviewing is a tool which will allow us to probe more deeply into the respondents' feelings, attitudes, orientations, hopes and fears. Interviews yield rich evidence that complements the generalizable but thin data from a questionnaire. If the questionnaire has produced unexpected or puzzling findings, we can explore them in depth through interviews.

Using a questionnaire to identify a subset of respondents for interview can raise problems over anonymity of findings. If the questionnaire is anonymous, how can we maintain our guarantee while identifying people who are willing to be interviewed?

There are two possibilities. First, we can breach the anonymity while offering reassurances. At the end of the questionnaire, after we have thanked them for their participation, we can include a brief statement that we intend to conduct follow-up interviews, and ask whether they would be willing to participate. If so, we will need to ask for a name and address or telephone number. Although this is relatively straightforward, it obviously means that our questionnaire is no longer anonymous.

A variation of this is illustrated by the *Travel Survey*. As an incentive to complete the questionnaire, we offered respondents the opportunity to enter a prize draw for a bicycle, which we thought an appropriate reward! The questionnaire had a tear-off strip, on which respondents were asked to give their name and details of how we could contact them if they had won. We reassured them that the slip would be detached from the questionnaire as soon as we had received it, and that all data would remain confidential.

If we decide that the questionnaire must remain anonymous, we shall have to supply respondents with two envelopes, one for their questionnaire and one for their personal details.

If the questionnaire is not anonymous, we are able to tie up each interview with the corresponding questionnaire. Should we do so? Should we refer back, in the interview, to the responses made on the questionnaire? At times, this can be fruitful, but care must be taken. We risk provoking socially desirable responses. If we continually remind respondents what they said before, they may adjust their replies to be consistent with that.

Using interviews, focus groups or diaries to suggest items for a questionnaire

Here the interviews, focus groups or diaries are being used less for their own sake than to help us formulate salient, meaningful questions for use in the questionnaire.

Triangulation

In the literature on research methods, **triangulation** refers to the use of a variety of research strategies, or of data from a variety of sources, to test an hypothesis. The term triangulation comes from surveying. We calculate the position of an object, C, by taking bearings on it from two positions, A and B. If we measure the distance between A and B, we know the length of one side of the triangle defined by points A, B, and C. We use an instrument such as a theodolite to measure the angle at apexes A and B. From this we can calculate the exact location of C. The point is, we need to make two or more independent measurements to do so.

But does this analogy stand up when dealing with social data? If we regard a questionnaire as a measurement from point A, and an interview as a measurement from point B, can we now determine point C – namely, data about a respondent? Are social data like that? If we ask a respondent about her opinions on field sports in an interview as well as a questionnaire, have we determined her opinions as definitively as we can calculate the location of an object in the landscape?

Perhaps not. One facet of social data, like quantum mechanics, is that the act of measurement affects the thing being measured. The accounts that people give in questionnaires, interviews, focus groups or diaries are just that: accounts. Whether it is possible to construct one objective, definitive statement out of these varying accounts is a contested philosophical question. Returning to the practical matters, we may simply conclude that an open-minded use of a variety of methods will do no harm, and will tend to enrich our understanding of the social world.

Key summary points

- Each method of data collection has advantages and disadvantages.
- Using more than one method is often desirable.

Points for reflection

- Would your research benefit if you combined methods of data gathering?
- Is there anything else you can do to increase the response rate?

Further reading

Devine and Heath (1999) *Sociological Research Methods in Context* is particularly useful in discussing the ways in which different research methods can be combined. Hornsby-Smith's chapter in Gilbert's (1993a) collection, *Researching Social Life*, provides a good account of the problems of access. Czaja and Blair (1995) *Designing Surveys: A Guide to Decisions and Procedures* is readable and wide ranging.

Selecting samples

Key elements in this chapter

- When sampling is necessary
- The differences between random (probability) sampling and the alternatives
- Theoretical and empirical populations
- The principles of probability sampling
- Types of probability design
- Sample size and sampling error
- Non-response
- The main types of non-probability selection

Introduction

Sampling is the process of choosing in a systematic fashion a sub-set of cases from which data will be collected from the pool of all those potentially relevant to the research being conducted. The sub-set selected is the **sample**, the pool is the **target population.** This terminology is used whatever the cases in question are – they will often be human individuals, but other possibilities in social science research include collectivities (households within a defined area, the stores within a retail chain), relationships (couples in the process of divorcing, doctors with patients who have a particular condition), events (inmate releases from prisons, patient 'episodes' in hospitals), or slices of space-time (urban intersections monitored over a period of time for possible accidents).

The need to make any type of selection always reflects researchers' limited resources. In an ideal world, data could be collected from every case in a target population (a situation sometimes referred to as **complete enumeration**). This is the objective, though never the achieved result, in some **censuses** conducted by nation states into the condition of their human populations. One hundred percent coverage of small target populations may be practical, but time constraints and finite budgets frequently render complete enumeration of large target populations out of the question. The researcher is then obliged to introduce some sort of selection of the cases to be included within the study. There is a fundamental choice to be made between the two major types of selection procedure. If data from the selected cases is to be used as the basis for generalizations about an entire target population then **probability** (or **random**) methods of sampling should be employed using the principles set out in the section devoted to this, below (page 62). If, on the other hand, data from the selected cases can stand in their own right and there is no requirement to generalize from them, the procedures set out in the section on non-probability sampling (page 79) will be adequate.

Whatever selection procedures are adopted, they need to be consistent with the overall project research design and should be developed in conjunction with the latter. Specifically, where the research design requires a comparison to be made between particular groups or time periods, then adequate quantities of cases with the appropriate attributes must be made available for the analysis stage by any selection procedures adopted. It is wise not to lose sight of the fact that even the most sophisticated sample design represents no more than an attempt to reach a rational compromise between rigour on the one hand and an effective application of time and money on the other. A further point is that even when 'scientific' sampling procedures are used under optimum conditions, all resulting generalizations derived from sample data are inevitably subject to a degree of error. The key advantage that probability sampling possesses over the alternative selection procedures is that it allows the likely size of this error to be calculated.

Sampling in a systematic fashion rests on relatively straightforward principles whose application in simple surveys is usually unproblematic. However, where a research problem seems to necessitate the construction of a complex sample design, the implications for the data analysis stage need to be checked out in advance with a statistician familiar with social surveys.

Theoretical populations

A consideration which is sometimes glossed over in methods texts but which needs to be given early attention in any but the purely descriptive survey concerns the definition of the target population. If a research project sets out to test a theoretical hypothesis or even, more modestly, to apply and explore theoretical concepts, there is then a need to consider what kinds of target population are relevant to the particular hypothesis or concepts. To ensure the adequate exploration of a theory, the empirical target population selected by the researcher needs to be included within the **theoretical population**, the usually infinite domain of empirical populations which any general theory addresses. This is essentially a conceptual consideration which needs to be dealt with at the research design stage.

Box 4.1   Ensuring a 'theoretically relevant' target population

In *Delinquent Boys: the Culture of the Gang* (1955), Cohen argued that gang delinquency was a response to the problems encountered by (largely) working class adolescents adjusting to a system of status evaluation operating in American society through which it was impossible for them to earn self-respect. The delinquent subculture represents an alternative status system built on an inversion of key middle class values, particularly respect for legitimately acquired possessions. The 'cavalier misappropriation or destruction of property' (Cohen 1955: 134) that it is argued is characteristic of much juvenile delinquency is interpreted as a rejection of middle class acquisition through diligence, self-discipline and sobriety and a celebration of their opposites.

A piece of research setting out to explore Cohen's ideas would need to begin by identifying a target population that is *theoretically relevant* to Cohen's thesis. A researcher based in Britain might be tempted to employ a target population of juveniles convicted for the offence of criminal damage and then move on to analyse the perpetrators' membership of peer groups and their class and school backgrounds. However, consideration would have to be given to whether the legal definition of criminal damage in the UK is sufficiently close to the 'cavalier misappropriation or destruction of property' for this population to be appropriate. An alternative approach might be to use the records of schools from a Local Education Authority area or areas to identify a target population of pupils who had committed acts of so-called 'mindless vandalism' in connection with school premises and property.

In either case, an additional issue is whether Cohen's theory was formulated in intrinsically culture-specific terms so that any fair test would have to be on an American target population. In general, the cases making up a target population should demonstrably possess the characteristics appropriate to the theory under scrutiny.

The discussion in Box 4.1 raises the general issue of the extent to which it is possible to test a theoretical hypothesis or explore theoretical concepts in a survey (or other research) which is not specifically designed for the task. Sometimes a theoretical framework can give rise to broad predictions or have corollaries that are sufficiently general to be confirmed or disconfirmed by the findings from general purpose survey or similar research. It could be the case in the example from Box 4.1 that data on the distribution of juvenile property crime across classes derived from existing official crime statistics are found to be at odds with Cohen's propositions. However, it is also possible that the outcome of this form of empirical test will be uncertain and contested because of (say) debate over whether the definitions of 'class' and 'property crime' that underpin the data are congruent with those offered by the theory. Specifically designed research generally offers the best chance of a decisive and rigorous test of a theory.

Probability sampling strategies

The main task in the remainder of this chapter is to outline the variety of strategies available for selecting a sample from the target population. Probability strategies will be dealt with first, followed by non-probability strategies.

Probability or random sampling is an integral feature of modern 'scientific' survey research (indeed, **scientific sampling** was an alternative name for it, though its use has now waned). Probability sampling is designed mainly to assist the accurate estimation of the values of characteristics of populations (**population parameters**) based on data obtained from a sample. Examples of typical parameters in which social researchers might be interested in relation to particular populations are the proportion of households that own a motor vehicle, and the average gross weekly income of economically active individuals. The term 'probability sampling' is a reference to the adoption of selection procedures which allow the use of inferences derived from the mathematical theory of probability. The link with this theory gives all probability selection strategies some unique features not enjoyed by any other ways of choosing the cases to supply data, though this is not to say it is universally appropriate or superior. Its special features are as follows:

- Probability selection cannot offer any cast-iron guarantee that a particular sample selected will be 'representative' of the mix of cases in the target population. Instead, it offers the researcher the possibility of calculating the level of likely **sampling error** associated with an estimate of a population value. Sampling error, which is discussed further below (page 76), can be thought of as the variability between every logically possible potential sample of a given size and type: the researcher (normally) selects just one.

- If the researcher can specify a desired level of accuracy for estimates of a key population value, the minimum necessary sample size to achieve it can be calculated. In other words, if the key population value the researcher wishes to know is (for example) the mean size of households within plus or minus 1 person, it is possible to work out how large the sample must be to deliver an estimate of this precision.
- It is a necessary condition for the use of a wide variety of statistical tests and measures at the data analysis stage.

Probability sampling requires the researcher to organize a lottery to determine which cases in the target population will make up the sample. There are, in fact, a few elaborations and qualifications on this but the essence of probability sampling is that it is designed to rule out the hand-picking of individual cases. 'Lottery' may well conjure up in the reader's mind images of flashing lights and a mechanical apparatus with revolving drums containing numbered celluloid balls. However, its use in connection with surveys is partly metaphorical: it indicates that the logical selection conditions present in a fair lottery must be simulated. No equipment is required and only a very limited form of lottery actually takes place.

As it applies in probability sampling, the selection lottery has to meet two general requirements. The first, and the more binding, states that every case in the target population should have a calculable and finite chance of inclusion in the sample. This implies that no case in the target population should be completely excluded and no case can be guaranteed inclusion in the sample in advance of selection. 'Finite' means here more than zero but less than 1: any case excluded from the outset would have a zero probability of inclusion in the sample – because an event that cannot happen has a probability of zero – while a case with a pre-set place in the sample would have a probability of 1, which in probability theory is the value associated with inevitable events. Surprise is sometimes expressed that the first principle is not more demanding. It does not state, as intuition expects, that every case be given an equal chance in the lottery. Why this is unnecessary is covered below, in the section on stratified random sampling. (Sample designs in which every case in the population has an equal chance of inclusion in the sample are, in fact, a special case and known as **epsem sample**s as an abbreviation of the phrase 'equal probability selection method'.)

The second principle requires that the selection of any case or group of cases takes place independently of the selection of any other individual case or group of cases. Drawing case number 128 in the target population for inclusion in the sample should have no bearing on the chances of number 252 (or any other case) getting selected subsequently. This requirement is less stringent than the first and probability theory as it applies to social surveys is sufficiently robust to allow it to be cautiously violated in tried and tested ways.

Two components are required to implement the selection lottery. The first is a sampling frame, which is a listing of all the cases in the relevant target population. Sometimes suitable listings are available ready-compiled, in other instances the compilation must be carried out by the researcher. One example of a pre-compiled sampling frame which has often been used to sample the 'general public' in the UK is the Electoral Register, which is a list of eligible voters listed by house number within each street and ward of a parliamentary constituency. It is prepared by local authority officials from returns submitted by householders and is held in each town hall. A second example is the PAF (Postcode Address File) which lists all the addresses in the United Kingdom by postcode and is produced by the Post Office. Since this is available in digital format, it has the advantage of being computer-searchable. Special variants of the PAF cover private households and institutions separately (although more detailed listings of business enterprises, specifying characteristics such as location, number of employees and sector of activity, can be purchased from business information brokers like Dun & Bradstreet Ltd). Other pre-compiled but more specialized sampling frames include the lists of registered members controlled by professional bodies, trade unions and enthusiast groups of various kinds.

The physical format of the sampling frame listing is incidental. In many cases it can be a 'virtual' list (thus the numbers 1 to 10 could stand for the ten administrative divisions of a state or region when listed in alphabetical order). The key requirements for any sampling frame are that it is comprehensive, accurate and up to date. However, despite the apparently straightforward character of a sampling frame, it needs to be emphasized that the task of creating one from scratch can be considerable for particular target populations: consider, for example, the problem of getting a national sample of discharged bankrupts or manufacturing organizations with exceptionally high degrees of workforce absenteeism. Sometimes the obstacles will be insuperable, in which case the research will have to be re-cast to employ a different target population, or it will have to be re-designed using a non-survey methodology.

The second requirement for implementing the lottery is a procedure for drawing the cases from the sampling frame. The procedure which corresponds most closely to probability theory is to use tables of random numbers. These are frequently included in the back of statistics texts and are simply collections of random digits where any digit is as likely to occur as any other and all combinations of digits are also equally likely. Computers can also generate random numbers for these purposes and most statistical packages include a convenient facility that allows you to specify a range within which you require the numbers to fall. The cases in the listing need to be numbered consecutively from 1 up to the total in the target population. Box 4.2 explains how to use printed random number tables.

Systematic selection is an alternative way to draw cases for the sample. If

---

Box 4.2   Using random number tables

Tables of random numbers are often presented as blocks of digits with intervening gaps to assist identification, but there is no significance to the number of digits included in the rows and columns. If the desired size of sample is (say) 550 cases, the task will be to select 550 instances of three consecutive digits between 001 and 550 inclusive from a numbered version of the sampling frame list. (You might actually need to select some 'spare' cases to cover contingencies such as refusals, failure to contact, and errors in the sampling frame.) The consecutive digits do not all have to be within a block of numbers. Note that the numbers assigned to each case in the sampling frame should actually or notionally be padded with leading zeros because within the random number tables, case 6 will be represented by the combination 006. So, in the example above, a three digit combination 044 in the table would be within range and the case assigned this number would be selected for the sample, but the combination 611 would be ignored as out of range and you would move on to the next set of three digits. You should nominate a starting position randomly (that is, without knowing what the first combinations of digits are). Then you can work through the random 'numbers' backwards or forwards by page, up or down blocks, including adjacent numbers or leaving gaps in any way that takes your fancy (provided you proceed consistently and accept and reject mechanically).

---

you require a sample of 500 cases from a population of 10,000, you would with this method simply select every twentieth case from the sampling frame. (The gap between selected cases is termed the **sampling fraction** or **sampling interval:** if the size of the population is represented by N and the size of the sample is represented by n, then the sampling interval $k = N/n$: in the example cited, $k = 10000/500 = 20$).

There are some additional considerations that surround the use of systematic selection. Your initial case should be selected at random (by, for example, using the random number generator of a computer statistics package with the range set to the sampling interval). If your sample is a large one (say, over 1000 cases), you should occasionally stop and make a new start with a case randomly chosen in the same manner as the first case. The reason for this is that a sampling frame could embody a concealed period or cycle within the listing of cases which coincides with your sampling interval. Suppose, for example, you are conducting a survey of residents on a housing estate and are sampling addresses. Unknown to you, every tenth address is associated with a corner plot containing a much larger house than the others. A sampling interval of ten could consistently catch every corner house and the resulting sample would significantly exaggerate the average income and overall affluence of households on the estate. A random starting point and periodic re-starts are designed to restrict the extent of any synchronization between the interval and the list. More generally, whenever a pre-compiled sampling frame is employed, it is important to know what principle has governed the ordering of cases on the list. Alphabetical order is usually 'neutral' for most research purposes (that is, unlikely to be connected with the key variables in a study), but the implications of chronological, geographical and 'exotic' ordering criteria need to be carefully examined.

If random re-starts are not used, systematic selection breaches the second (independence) principle of the selection lottery in that the choice of the first case effectively determines the identity of all the rest of the cases that make up a particular sample. However, it is often the most convenient procedure to implement and provided that the sampling frame is ordered on a neutral principle and periodic re-starts are employed, selection of cases by sampling interval approximates reasonably closely to the rigour of full random selection. In the sub-sections that follow, particular probability sample designs and refinements are examined in sufficient detail to assist the reader to recognize the appropriateness of each variant to different kinds of research situation. Details of more comprehensive treatments of sample design are given in the further reading section at the end of the chapter.

Simple random sampling (SRS)

In this design, the cases that will make up the sample are chosen in a single process of selection from the sampling frame that covers the entire target population. If the cases are numbered from 1 to N in advance, selection can be based on random number tables. The question of how to determine the appropriate sample size is dealt with on page 77.

Stratified random sampling

Stratification is an important refinement of the selection process which, operating under suitable conditions, can improve upon the effectiveness of SRS sampling. It requires the identification of a 'stratifying variable' (occasionally several variables) on the basis of whose values the target population can be divided into distinctive 'strata' or groupings. A separate random sample is then taken from each stratum. Normally, it has to be possible to determine the value of every case in the target population on the stratifying variable(s) before selecting the sample. Thus, stratification requires the researcher to acquire some information about the target population under study in advance of data collection (for instance, from previous research) and it exploits this additional information to build a sample that

---

Box 4.3   A simple random sample of customers

A utility company decides to survey its 16,400 private customers in one of its operating regions to establish the effectiveness of its customer relations. It is decided that an SRS sample of roughly 2000 will be adequate. The comprehensive list of customer names for the region is extracted from the computer database used for billing and the names are transferred to a spreadsheet and allocated consecutive numbers starting from 00001 and ending at 16400. A random sample of 2000 numbers falling in the range between 1 and 16400 inclusive is generated by the spreadsheet and the corresponding customers are selected.

This sample of customers will provide a systematic basis for making generalizations about all the customers in the region. However, there will inevitably be variation between the very large number of different samples of 2000 cases that could be generated by this selection procedure. As a result, generalizations based on the sample data will be subject to a probable degree of error that can be calculated.

Conducting a SRS of all the customers offers no guarantee, as was made clear on page 64, that the resulting sample will be representative of particular types that exist in the target population. It is unlikely to contain (for instance) exactly the same proportion of female customers, new customers, small volume users, or late payers as there are in the region. If it is important to ensure that the sample reflects the proportions of cases with key characteristics in the target population, or that it contains a minimum number of such cases, refinements to the sample design are needed.

An additional point with large target populations is that paper listings will be bulky and difficult to handle, so some form of 'virtual' computer listing will usually be preferable.

---

mirrors the composition of the target population on the chosen characteristic(s). In choosing a stratifying variable, the essential requirement is that cases in each 'stratum' (that is, with the same value of the stratifying variable) should have similar relationships with the dependent variable(s) of interest in the study, but that as much variability as possible should exist between strata and the dependent variable(s). The gains from introducing stratification increase to the extent that this requirement is met.

Consider an example. In an organizational study of job satisfaction (the dependent variable), *job grade* would be an appropriate stratifying variable provided that membership of different job grades significantly affected levels of job satisfaction. (There might be evidence on this in the literature). If the values of job grade were, 'Management', 'Technical and supervisory staff', 'Shop floor staff', the target population would in this case be divided into these three strata. Lists of the members in the groupings could be obtained from the Personnel Department and would constitute three sampling frames from each of which cases would be chosen in turn by a random procedure. Some variation between the levels of job satisfaction of individuals within the shop floor stratum and within the other strata would, of course, remain – if there was none left at all, there would be little for the research to reveal! The requirement for stratification to work beneficially is simply that there should be less within-stratum variation than between-stratum variation.

The next matter that needs to be settled is what sampling fraction should be used for each stratum. In the simplest case, where the design is referred to as **proportionate stratified sampling** (PSS), a uniform fraction is used for all the strata. This results in a sample which is a mirror of the target population with respect to the stratifying variable. Each grouping of the stratifying variable constitutes the same proportion of the sample as it does of the population. The alternative, **disproportionate stratified sampling** (DSS), varies the sampling fraction for different strata. There are several reasons for doing this. One is simply to increase the representation in the final sample of small strata which otherwise might contribute only a handful of cases from which no sound inferences could be drawn. Another reason is to deliberately divert extra research resources to strata known in advance to have highly variable relationships with respect to the key dependent variable, at the expense of strata known in advance to have relatively homogeneous relationships with this variable. In the research on job satisfaction, for example, it might be known from a previous survey that technical and supervisory staff were, as a group, characterized by especially variable and fluctuating levels of job satisfaction in comparison to shop floor staff where the levels were more consistent between individuals and over time. Directing extra sample cases to the most variable stratum in a sample design from less variable strata can be an extremely effective way of reducing overall sampling error.

The DSS sample in column (4) of Table 4.1 now provides a better basis for making generalizations about Management and Technical and supervisory staff than the SRS design in column (2) or the PSS design in column (3) without using a larger sample. As it stands, however, the composition of the DSS sample in terms of strata might now seem to be in danger of giving a distorted picture of the target population as a whole. The remedy is to give each case in the sample a numerical weighting (based on the sampling fraction) which returns both over-sampled strata and under-sampled strata to their true proportions in the population: this weighting can be used throughout the data analysis stage.

This capacity to re-weight data explains why the lottery principles do not need to insist on giving all the cases (and groups of cases) in the target population equal chances of inclusion in the sample. The choice between feeding weighted or unweighted data into analyses is an option provided in most computer survey packages.

Box 4.4   A comparison of SRS, PSS and DSS

This box explores sampling designs for the organizational study of job satisfaction introduced on page 69. A study of job satisfaction seeks to conduct
interviews with a cross-section of all the personnel in an organization with
the available resources keeping the limit to 100 interviews. Column (1) in
Table 4.1 below shows the size of each stratum and the target population.
Column (2) indicates the situation using a simple random sample (SRS)
with a sampling fraction of 1 in 50. The question marks indicate that the
strata play no role in the SRS selection process and indicate the uncertainty
over exactly how many cases there will actually be in the sample from each
category. Column (3) shows the results of using a proportionate stratified
sample (PSS) with the same 1 in 50 sampling fraction as column (2) but
selected from each stratum separately. One obvious problem with adopt-
ing a uniform sampling fraction in this instance is that it would provide too
few cases for study from the smaller strata.

Column (4) shows the results from a disproportionate stratified sample
(DSS) that varies the sampling fraction for the different strata. The objective
in this instance would be partly to increase the numbers in the final sample
from both the management and technical staff strata, but also to deliberately over-sample technical staff where job satisfaction is likely to be highly
variable. The shop floor staff are 'under-sampled' in comparison to their
proportion in the population while the other two groups are 'over-sampled'
at the expense of the former. Provided the assumptions about variations in
job satisfaction are correct, the sampling error for (4) should be less than
that for either (2) or (3) despite the sample size remaining constant.

Table 4.1   Comparison of SRS, PSS and DSS designs

Stratum	(1) Population N	(2) SRS 1:50	(3) PSS 1:50	(4) DSS proportion	n
Management	250	?	5	1:8.3	30
Technical	500	?	10	1:12.5	40
Shop floor	4250	?	85	1:141.6	30
Total	5000	100	100	1:50	100

Part of the importance of stratification in probability sampling is that it is
the principal means by which the researcher can engineer what is popularly
thought of as a 'representative' sample. Unless there is stratification by
gender, household size, or average rent etc., then there is no control in

probability sampling of the manner in which specific characteristics and attributes of cases appear in the sample. It follows that for practical reasons representativeness is something that can only be achieved for a small number of specific characteristics and not globally for the sample as a whole.

Box 4.5   Combining stratification and systematic selection

A straightforward way to implement stratification in conjunction with systematic selection is to sort the cases in the sampling frame into order by ascending or descending value of the stratifying variable (or variables). The table below shows an extract from a sampling frame adapted from the UK Post Office's Postcode Address File.

Sampling unit	% owner occupiers
Region I	
Postal sector 1356	64
Postal sector 1456	60
Postal sector 1567	56
etc . . .	
Region 2	
Postal sector 2345	48
Postal sector 2456	47
Postal sector 2567	47
etc . . .	

Postal sectors are areas made up of adjacent postal codes. In order to achieve national coverage, this sample is stratifying by region. In order to achieve a range of socio-economic backgrounds, it is also stratifying by percentage of owner occupier households, a figure available for small areas from census data. Provided a suitable sampling interval is chosen, selection of sectors from each region and a range of socio-economic backgrounds can be guaranteed. This box can be read in conjunction with Box 4.6.

Multi-stage sampling

A second major refinement of SRS designs entails the possibility of conducting several stages of selection in sequence. An example will simplify the explanation. A research project may necessitate data collection from a very large, perhaps national, target population. It may well be the case that no national sampling frame exists (and even if one did, it would be extremely time-consuming to set up an SRS design in conjunction with it). It is also possible, however, that adequate sampling frames may be available for localities. Large scale populations are invariably organized into a variety of hierarchical units. In the case of a nation state like the United Kingdom, one set of hierarchical units could be *administrative region, parliamentary constituency, borough, ward, street address,* and *household.* The units are hierarchical in as much as lower units are 'nested' within higher ones: every street address 'belongs to' a ward, and every ward fits into a borough, and so on. Sampling procedures are able to make use of this arrangement by moving down the hierarchy making selections from each unit in turn until they are able to exploit existing sampling frames or it is feasible to create them. In the example given, starting at the 'top' of the system, the **primary sampling unit** or **PSU** would be the administrative region. A sub-set of regions would be chosen using random procedures and the parliamentary constituencies they contained would be listed to make up the sampling frame for the second stage (so that the secondary sampling unit or SSU would be the constituency). Random selection would again take place and the boroughs in the chosen constituencies would be listed to form the sampling frame for the third stage, and so on. An important 'economy' in the procedure is that only selected units are passed on from each stage reducing the size of the next sampling frame that has to be constructed. There is no theoretical limit to the number of stages in a design although each process of selection adds cumulatively to the overall sampling error. It is possible to combine multi-stage sampling with stratification and other refinements to produce sophisticated designs.

Box 4.6   The Family Expenditure Survey (FES) – a complex national sampling design

The FES is an annual sample survey of private households' spending and saving that has been conducted in the UK by the Office of Population Census and Surveys (OPCS) and the Office of National Statistics (ONS) since 1957. The achieved sample size is about 7000 and respondents complete expenditure diaries as well as taking part in interviews. The key features from a sampling viewpoint are as follows:

- the design is a two-stage, stratified and clustered, random sample;
- the sampling frame is the Post Office's small users' Postcode Address File;
- there are various exclusions including offshore islands (owing to the expense of collection), members of the US armed forces, Roman Catholic priests living in parish accommodation, and households containing members of the diplomatic service of other countries – though non-British households are not generally excluded: Northern Ireland is covered but the sampling arrangements differ from those described here;

- the PSU is a *postal sector* – ward-sized areas which provide the clustering element in the design: 672 sectors are selected at stage 1, 10,000 addresses are selected at stage two;
- sectors are stratified by (1) Government Office region to give a geographical spread, (2) whether an area is officially classified as urban or not to cover urban–rural differences, (3) the proportion of owner occupiers and the proportion of renters according to the last census to ensure a socio-economic spread. For further details, see ONS (annually) *Family Spending*. The URL is: http://www.statistics.gov.uk/products/

Cluster samples are a specialized adaptation of multi-stage designs. A major component of the expense of surveys based on household or work-based interviews is the travel costs incurred conveying interviewers to respondents, especially where the target population is widely distributed geographically. A procedure for reducing costs by concentrating the data collection operation is to divide the area covered by the target population into a number of clusters of adjacent cases, perhaps circumscribed by district or other geographical boundaries for which sampling frames exist. The list of clusters is then sampled randomly and the chosen clusters are translated into the final sampling unit, usually addresses. All the cases in chosen clusters (or, at a minimum, a substantial proportion of them) are included in the sample. With the addresses of selected individuals or households bunched together, field workers need to travel to fewer disparate locations and can conduct more interviews per trip. The logic of cluster sampling means that it works best where each cluster is as heterogeneous as possible. Ideally, each cluster would approach the diversity of the target population as a whole and in this respect desirable characteristics for a cluster are the opposite of those in stratification where there is a premium on homogeneity within a stratum. Clustering is an example of a refinement that is designed primarily to reduce costs in a way that minimizes the impact on sampling errors, but it will still normally be the case that sampling error is higher in a cluster sample than in a SRS of the same size.

A potential problem with multi-stage sampling is that it can lead to difficulties producing a sample of the desired size owing to potential differences in the size of the PSUs. A useful device that is commonly employed to deal with this is to arrange for the selection of PSUs with **probability proportional to size** (PPS). The chance of selection for each PSU is adjusted so that it is proportional to the number of cases in the target population that each PSU contains. Further details are given in Box 4.7.

Box 4.7 Implementing probability proportional to size for a multi-stage design

A convenient way to apply PPS is to construct a table for all the PSUs in the target population with the cumulative number of cases they represent. In this example, the PSUs are nine regions with the following populations:

PSU	Size	Cumulative size
Region 1	1 100 000	1 100 000
Region 2	250 000	1 350 000
Region 3	980 000	2 330 000
Region 4	190 000	2 520 000
Region 5	490 000	3 010 000
Region 6	3 600 000	6 610 000
Region 7	1 300 000	7 910 000
Region 8	1 000 000	8 910 000
Region 9	1 090 000	10 000 000

Assuming random number tables are to be used and four regions need to be selected for stage 2, the task becomes one of drawing four lots of four digits ranged between 0001 and 1000 (the final four zeros in the cumulative size column can be ignored). Any set of four digits drawn from the tables between 0001 and 0110 inclusive will select Region 1, between 0111 and 0135 inclusive will select Region 2, between 0136 and 0233 inclusive will select Region 3, etc., etc. Region 3 is represented by 98 sets of digits, as against the 49 sets available for Region 5 which has half its population. Thus the number of sets of digits that correspond to a region (and therefore the chances of any region being selected) is proportional to the size of its population.

   Note that care needs to be taken to ensure that the selection units and procedures employed in subsequent stages do not 'undo' the proportionality created in stage 1.

Accuracy, precision and confidence intervals

Little mention has so far been made of sample size. The question of how large a particular sample needs to be cannot always yield a simple direct answer. To be clear about the issues surrounding size, it is necessary to return again to the probability basis of sampling and, as a preliminary, to introduce the distinction between **accuracy** and **precision**. As we have seen, random selection procedures generate samples the data from which can be used to estimate the value of selected population characteristics. It is not possible, however, to establish exactly the accuracy of an estimate, that is, how closely a specific estimate based on an executed sample coincides with the true population value. What the statistics of probability sampling do instead is to make it possible to calculate the precision of an estimate. Precision indicates how closely the estimates derived from all the samples of a given size and design that could possibly be selected from the target population cluster around the population value being predicted. Precision is measured by the family of **standard error** statistics, one of which exists for every individual estimator (thus, there is a standard error of the mean, a standard error of a proportion, etc.). Calculations of precision take the form of confidence intervals. The *interval* element is a range of values centred on the sample estimate within which the population value is predicted to fall: the *confidence* element refers to a level of certainty attached to the prediction, conventionally 95 per cent or 99 per cent. If the researcher wishes to be 99 per cent confident in the prediction, the range of values the interval covers will be larger (and therefore the estimate will be less precise) than if he or she settles for the 95 per cent level. Several of the textbooks cited at the end of the chapter set out the statistics for calculating confidence intervals in detail.

Sample size and sampling error

It has been noted (page 64) that sampling error was a measure of the overall variability between every possible sample of a particular size and design that could be selected from a target population. The greater the sampling error associated with a sample, the lower the precision of the estimates produced from it. Increasing the sample size represents one way of reducing sampling error and improving precision, but it is rather inefficient because sampling error varies with the square of sample size (in SRS samples). In other words, in order to halve the level of sampling error, the sample size must be increased four times. Modification of the overall research design and/or refinement of the sample design (through, for example, stratification) may be preferable to conducting a large and potentially expensive sampling and data gathering operation.

It is possible to obtain a concrete indication of the scale of sampling error for a particular type of sample design. Consider a dichotomous (yes/no) variable such as 'households who have spent a holiday abroad within the last five years' which available evidence might suggest is split about 50–50 in the population, the worst case from a sampling viewpoint. The sampling error for this attribute would be just over ±3 per cent in SRS samples of 1000 at the 95 per cent level of confidence. This means that if there were 52 per cent in the sample who had taken foreign holidays, we could be 95 per cent sure that there were between 49 per cent and 55 per cent in the population. If the sample size could be increased to 2500, the sampling error would fall to 2 per cent and the confidence interval would shrink to between 50 per cent and 54 per cent.

How can the appropriate size for a sample be determined? If a project has as a key objective the estimation of the value of a particular population parameter with a particular level of precision and confidence (say, for example, the average household income in a particular target population plus or minus £10 at 95 per cent confidence), then it is relatively straight-forward in SRS samples to work out exactly how large the sample needs to be to produce this (see, for example, the calculations in Kalton 1966, pp. 24–5, or Moser and Kalton 1971, section 7.1). In many cases (as above with foreign holidays), such calculations require a preliminary estimate of the variability of the key parameter within the population. However, because most projects have diffuse objectives, the appropriate level of precision to set and the variables to prioritize are not always self-evident. Some analysis will invariably be based on selected sub-groups where the numbers will be smaller and the sampling errors will be higher than when the sample as a whole is under consideration. The conventional strategy is to err on the side of caution and base sampling error considerations on the least favourable variables, those likely to have the highest variability in the target population. A rule of thumb also sometimes offered is not to permit the size of any sub-group which will be the basis of analysis to fall below 50.

Other types of error that affect surveys

A distinction is often drawn between the different types of inaccuracy or error that can affect surveys depending on their source because what needs to be done about them varies. As their name implies, **selection errors** origi-nate in the selection process itself while **non-selection errors** are the residual category which come from anywhere else in survey methodology (and which will not be discussed further here). The most serious types of selection and non-selection errors are listed in Table 4.2 together with likely responses to them (though the optimum response depends on the point at which a prob-lem comes to light).

Sampling error was discussed in the last section. Considering the other types of selection error in Table 4.2, a degree of sampling frame inaccuracy may be inevitable and where a list is compiled by an external agency, a researcher may have no option other than to accept its limitations and take them into account in the research design. The incorrect inclusion of cases which are not properly a genuine part of the target population may subse-quently come to light and be self-correcting (for instance, on contact with

Table 4.2 Types of error in surveys

Selection problems	Possible responses
Sampling error too large	Increase sample size, refine sample design
Sampling frame flaws	Checks to establish extent of problems
Non-response	Reminders (postal surveys) or recalls (Telephone and household interviews)

Non-selection problems	Possible responses
Use of incorrect or biased estimator	Consult statistician
Interviewer mistakes	Simplify interview schedule, re-instruct interviewers
Coding errors	Use computer-verified data entry; revise coding schemes

respondents), whereas the omission from the frame of cases which should have been included is more serious because it is less likely to be discovered automatically. Non-response is a fundamental problem that affects most surveys to a greater or lesser extent. It refers to the failure of research efforts to gather data from all the cases that genuinely belong in the sample. Reasons for non-response include the refusal or inability of respondents to participate and cases which turn out to be uncontactable (on account of the death or relocation of individuals, their change of status, or the closure of businesses, etc). If non-response reaches high levels, it can threaten the statistical validity of survey findings. It is quite distinct from sampling error: by definition, sampling error is a random variation between possible samples, but non-response is highly unlikely to be random. Respondent refusals to participate in surveys, for example, are likely to come disproportionately from certain social groups. These include those who have unorthodox views on the topics of the research (or who simply believe their views to be unorthodox) and who can be especially reluctant to reveal them. Individuals who are socially excluded or have conflictual relationships with agencies of social control are especially likely to refuse irrespective of the nature of the research in question. This element of self-selection means that the responders/achieved cases cannot be taken as representative of the non-responders/non-achieved cases. In much the same way, individuals who prove difficult to contact will possibly have occupations and life-styles substantially different to those of respondents.

The classic remedy for dealing with the non-contact element of non-response in postal questionnaires is postal (or telephone) reminders. In household interviewing, the procedures can require a fixed number of call-backs to an address at different times to the original visit. Refusals can be dealt with by a variety of methods including incentive payments or other rewards and careful prior attention to the design of covering letters and preparatory information. Another tack that can be adopted when persuasion to participate has failed is to try to get at least one piece of non-contentious information from refusers (such as age) so that it is possible to compare their profile with that of respondents on a variable common to both.

Non-selection errors are included in Table 4.2 for completeness and are discussed in the sections on data collection and coding. The variety of sources of error discussed above underlines the reluctance of experienced survey researchers to rely wholly on large samples to deliver high precision estimates since increasing sample size reduces only sampling error but does not deal with the other sources.

Box 4.8   The *Travel Survey*: sample design

The *Travel Survey* addressed two different target populations of commuters, students and staff. The student target population was restricted to those in the second or subsequent year of their courses since a very high proportion of first years lived in halls of residence on the campus itself. Only staff working on the main campus were included. It was decided to use a DSS approach: the sampling fraction for most of the staff was set to 1:4 as against 1:5 for students because staff commuting was a more critical problem. Staff from three departments scheduled to move to a new campus were oversampled with a 1:3 fraction. The designated target populations were 4763 staff and 7995 students. The designated sample size was 1220 staff and 1998 students. The achieved sample sizes were 590 staff (48%) and 282 students (14%).

Sampling strategies: non-probability sampling

Non-probability selection methods do not implement a random selection lottery. They cannot therefore make use of inferences from probability theory and, in consequence, they do not provide equivalent guarantees of precision to the procedures discussed in the previous sections. They nevertheless may have a specialist role to play at particular stages of the survey process.

Convenience sampling

A convenience sample, as the name implies, is based on a selection of cases which are easily accessible to the researcher for the expenditure of relatively little effort. Examples of high accessibility are households located in neighbourhoods close to the researcher's residence, or students in the researchers' own classes. The element of deliberate selection by the researcher and the fact of his or her association with the chosen cases seriously compromises these types of selection. Even where the cases are neither local nor personally known to the researcher, the 'convenience' of selecting them may be connected to the fact that they are celebrated or long-established instances of their class and, in these respects, atypical of the target population as a whole. The use of convenience samples should properly be restricted to feasibility studies and pilot research. Even here, their utility is problematic unless they are made up of cases with similar attributes to the target population. If not, the information they produce will be of little use even to test out the suitability of survey arrangements or instrumentation.

Snowball sampling

In this variant, the researcher relies on each case to supply details of the location of further cases, so that the sample grows steadily in extent (metaphorically, like a snowball rolled along the snowy ground). It is appropriate in somewhat specialized circumstances which may be summarized as follows:

- no sampling frame exists;
- cases are rare and are geographically widely distributed;
- cases are likely to know of each other;
- cases are willing to supply information about each other.

Circumstances in which snowball sampling might prove useful are where there is a need to gather together a collection of organizations offering a very new service or product (and which are likely to be aware of the competitors), or patients (or possibly relatives of patients) suffering from rare medical conditions who may be in contact with fellow sufferers. In situations where the condition or characteristic is socially undesirable, however, referrals may not be forthcoming. Snowball samples suffer from the same main limitations as convenience samples and their use is generally limited to exploratory studies.

Purposive sampling

Purposive sampling is employed mainly in exploratory and in qualitative research. The logic of this kind of selection is not based on *typicality* but on locating cases with attributes of particular interest to the researcher. An implementation of purposive sampling is contained within the 'grounded theory' approach discussed in Glaser and Strauss (1967), Strauss (1987) and Strauss and Corbin (1993). Together with some of the other purposive selection procedures, grounded theory is preoccupied with the creation of explanatory categories and, through them, with building theoretical systems, rather than with demonstrating that cases are representative of their empirical populations. In order to construct such categories, the researcher seeks a collection of paradigmatic or 'ideal' instances, extreme examples, recent or old instances, instances where x occurs with y or in the absence of z, etc. From the viewpoint of selection, the two key elements in grounded theory are (i) theoretical sampling, '. . . whereby the analyst decides on analytic grounds what data to collect next and where to find them' (Strauss 1987, 38); and (ii) sampling to saturation, where data from cases with the desired attributes are collected at a research site up to the point at which no new insights or further information is uncovered. Such an approach allows data gathered early to be analysed in time to influence subsequent data selection and gathering strategies.

The objectives of purposive sampling are radically different from those of probability sampling and it cannot be judged by the same criteria. Clearly, however, like convenience and snowball techniques, it does not allow the calculation of levels of precision.

Quota sampling

Quota sampling is widely used in market research and opinion polling in circumstances where probability sampling would also be appropriate. It requires researchers to be able to estimate in advance how key variables (usually demographic attributes like age and sex) are distributed in the target population. From this information, quotas of interlocking attributes that respondents must satisfy are devised and given to interviewers. The accumulated totals of all the quotas reflect the proportions of the characteristics in the population. The interviewers then have some discretion about finding suitable respondents to fulfil the quota within their allocated neighbourhoods. Some assignments allow for street interviewing, others for household interviewing only. An example quota that could be assigned to an interviewer is given in Table 4.3. In this example, the interviewer needs to find (among others) three women who are in the 45–64 age bracket and are all in the lower occupational class. If household interviews were being conducted, some restrictions like one person per household, no adjacent addresses, might be applied.

A quota sample can be regarded as an attempt to combine the advantages of stratification (introduced via the interlocking characteristics) with a degree of clustering (the result of each interviewer operating within a particular location or neighbourhood). Their attraction to commercial organizations is that they are relatively easy to set up quickly with the clustering offering savings on overheads like travel and subsistence. Comparisons of probability and quota samples suggest that the latter can, in knowledgeable

Table 4.3 Interlocking sex, age and occupational class characteristics of respondents

Class	Prof/Managerial		Intermediate		Lower		Totals
	Male	Female	Male	Female	Male	Female	
Age 20–29	1	–	–	1	1	1	4
30–34	–	1	–	1	3	1	6
45–64	–	–	1	1	2	3	7
65+	–	–	–	–	1	2	3
Totals	1	1	1	3	7	7	20

hands, offer equivalent accuracy despite the fact that the interviewer's greater discretion in quota sampling is an additional potential source of errors. However, quota samples do not permit sampling errors to be calculated in the same way they are for probability samples and, overall, the technique is better suited to team research conducted by experienced practitioners than it is to solo or novice surveyors.

Key summary points

- Sampling is a means through which compromises can be reached between rigour and getting the most out of finite research resources.
- Random sampling offers important advantages if you wish to generalize from your results.
- Deliberate selection, or opportunities for self-selection, of respondents is usually a serious threat to random samples.
- It is difficult or impossible to modify many sampling procedures in mid-stream, for example, to take advantage of unexpected early results.

Points to reflect on

- What from research considerations alone, would represent an ideal target population? What characteristics would the cases in it possess?
- Is your sample design practical? Can it be implemented in the time-scale and with the resources you have available?
- Is your sample design consistent with your overall research design?
- If you are depending on a pre-existing sampling frame, will its owners permit you to use it? Do you know how and why it was compiled and understand what its limitations are?

Further reading

Chapters 5 and 6 of Moser and Kalton (1971) *Survey Methods in Social Investigation* (2nd edn) are written at an introductory level and include only the minimum of statistical theory. Kalton's (1983) *Introduction to Survey Sampling* (out of print but still available in academic libraries) offers a compact, intermediate level, treatment. A more recent alternative to Kalton is Barnett (1991). Kish (1965) offers an advanced theoretical handbook on sampling principles.

(5) Collecting your data

Doing it yourself

In large-scale surveys, data collection is typically contracted out to an agency which employs hired hands. They conduct the interviews, if there are any. They code the responses and enter them into the computer. In contrast to this supposed drudgery, the creative work of design and analysis is done by the researchers.

This book is addressed to people who are collecting the data themselves, either individually or as a member of a small research team. Doing it yourself has a number of advantages, particularly for interviewing, as Saunders (1990: 383) argues in his survey of home owners.

First, doing it yourself gives you a far better 'feel' for the data than if a hired interviewer had simply delivered the findings to you. You will know not only what was said but how it was said. You will have an insight into what areas respondents found sensitive, and why this was so. You will also be better able to judge which items were the most salient to respondents.

Second, hired interviewers are not necessarily interested in the research. Why should they be, especially if we have defined them as the muscle and ourselves as the brains? The pay is poor, and it is piecework – so the quicker they can get through an interview the better it will be for them. To make the interview go smoothly, they may say things which the researchers certainly would not have sanctioned. Aldridge recently had the experience of being interviewed by someone who complimented him on his taste in classical music, which she deduced from the CDs on display in his sitting room. The interviewer proceeded to agree with some of his answers! Flattering, perhaps, but very damaging to validity.

Whether or not hired interviewers deviate from our script, their situation encourages an instrumental and calculative approach to the interviews. Because of this, researchers on large-scale surveys have to spend days on the recruitment and training of interviewers, and on making the interview schedule's instructions watertight.

Third, using hired interviewers is feasible only where interviews are highly structured. If we want to ask searching open-ended questions, it is better to do so ourselves.

We would add two more points, implicit in what Saunders says. Doing it yourself is deeply satisfying. It is also more conducive to the exercise of the sociological imagination.

Commissioned research

Many readers will be carrying out research for someone else: an employer, a voluntary association, a church or charity. Even though you are doing it yourself, and whether or not you are being paid, you do not have a free hand.

It may be the sponsor's view that they have the aim and the vision, while you have the technical know-how. Paradoxically, however, sponsors are usually surprisingly vague about what they want to know. Nor do they necessarily have a clear strategy for the research – they simply want to commission 'a survey'.

This means that you will be involved in discussion with your sponsors to establish not just the practical details of the survey but its objectives. Your role is to help the sponsors clarify what it is they want to know. Sponsors usually recognize this soon after negotiations begin. At this stage, they are open to your proposals about how to define and achieve the objectives of the research.

Difficulties with sponsors tend to arise later. The survey method can be a victim of its own virtue, its openness to public scrutiny. Sponsors will ask to see your draft questionnaire or interview schedule. Two things tend to happen. They will ask you to modify or omit some questions as too sensitive, and they will present you with questions they want you to include. These requests may come very late, and just at the time when you are ready to launch the survey having completed your **piloting**.

If you are asked to modify or omit questions, it shows that the sponsor is probably afraid of the answers. This is a sign that we should be asking exactly those questions. Even though sponsors say their objective is to improve their service to their clients, they may be frightened by the prospect of a barrage of criticism. In a large organization, one section – the catering department, say – may feel it is being unduly exposed to criticism. They may well say that they have done their own 'survey' already, and know all they need to know.

When you are asked to include questions, the problem is that the sponsor usually expects you to include them word for word. *This* is what they want to know, and *this* is how they want you to ask it. If the questions are well designed there will be no problem; but what chance is there of that? One or two badly worded questions can seriously damage the overall quality of the responses and the response rate itself.

How to handle this? Clearly, the answer depends on the precise situation. We suggest one principle: emphasize the technicalities. You have been asked to carry out a survey because you have expertise. Even if you are a beginner, reading this book will give you far more knowledge about surveys than your sponsors have. They have asked for your advice, and you should not be apologetic about it. If you helped them in the early stages to clarify their objectives, they are likely to follow your advice now.

Questionnaires and structured interview schedules are documents that sponsors can ask to vet. Such scrutiny of the details is not so easy in the case of unstructured interviews and focus groups. This is one reason for including them in our research strategy: they are less vulnerable to the sponsor's attentions.

Covering letters for postal questionnaires

A postal questionnaire must be accompanied by a covering letter. There is no formula for such letters – as ever, the sociological imagination comes into play. How the letter is worded will depend on the topic of the research, the respondents, your relationship with the respondents, and what you are able and willing to promise as regards feedback. Box 5.1 offers some guidelines.

If the resources are available, it is worth sending a reminder letter to those who have not responded. Doing so invariably generates a significant number

Box 5.1 Guidelines for a covering letter

Style The letter should be clear, straightforward, businesslike and fairly formal, but not pompous. Headed writing paper is helpful. An informal chatty style will be off-putting to some respondents, who will read it as frivolous. On the other hand, the days are happily gone when we could address respondents self-importantly, as though they were obliged to take part.

Spelling and grammar Like it or not, many people interpret mistakes in spelling and grammar as signs that the writer is careless, ill-educated or unintelligent. However unfair, these judgements will be made, to the detriment of the response rate and the quality of responses. Do proof read carefully, and ask for advice if you need to.

Purposes of the research We need to say as much as we can about this – but as briefly as possible – in order to persuade respondents that participation is worthwhile. We may need to mention sponsorship or funding, and should also give a concise statement about our position as researchers.

How the respondent was selected Unless it is obvious from the context of the research, we should explain briefly and non-technically how the respondent was selected for inclusion in the study.

Why the respondent can help Sometimes respondents fear they cannot help us because they are not experts and do not know enough about our research topic. We may need to reassure them about this, for example by saying that we are interested in their opinions and experience, and that we wish to have a broad coverage of all shades of opinion.

Confidentiality and anonymity We need to be clear about what guarantees we are giving, and to be alert to the problem that some respondents may take confidentiality to mean anonymity. If the questionnaire has a serial number, we should explain its significance.

Feedback We may decide to offer feedback individually to respondents, though this can be costly. Alternatively, we may indicate to them where our findings will be published. One possibility is to use the world wide web.

Answering queries It may be desirable to give a telephone number or email address which respondents can use if they have any queries.

Thanks We should thank the respondent in anticipation of their taking part.

of extra responses. It works more easily when the questionnaires are not anonymous, since we can target the reminders to non-respondents.

As with a covering letter, there is no formula for a reminder. Clearly, people are entitled to refuse, so we cannot be accusatory in tone. What we should do is refer to the value of the research and of the respondent's participation.

Box 5.2   Guidelines for a reminder letter

Keep it short A reminder letter should be even shorter than the original covering letter.

Content Refer to the value of the respondent's participation.

Facilitation Enclose another copy of the questionnaire and another stamped addressed envelope.

Appreciation Acknowledge that the respondent's reply may be in the post, and thank the respondent.

Box 5.3 shows the text of the covering letter used in the *Travel Survey*. As is normal in real life research, the outcome was a compromise. Although drafted by the Survey Unit it went out over the signature of the senior academic responsible for traffic on campus. Given the context of the research, it was thought essential to explain the reasons why the university was conducting a survey.

Box 5.3   An example of a covering letter

Professor David Greenaway
Pro-Vice-Chancellor and Professor of Economics
Department of Economics
University Park
Nottingham NG7 2RD

Dear Colleague/Student,

Travel to Work Survey 1998

Thank you for finding time to complete this questionnaire.

Why are we doing it?

The University is committed to traffic management policies aimed at reducing vehicle dependency, encouraging the use of public transport and managing vehicular movements within and between our campuses. This commitment is part of a wider environmental strategy for the University. The survey will identify the travel patterns of staff and students that will assist us in formulating policies to:

- tackle the problems of increasing demand for vehicular access and parking;
- make recommendations for developing and supporting viable and accessible transport alternatives.

The findings of the survey will be reported to Transport Consultants who will advise us in producing a Commuter Plan for the University, which is expected in October 1998.

About the survey

The survey is confidential. If you complete and return the questionnaire accompanied by the slip below you can be entered into a prize draw to win a bicycle. There will be two prizes, one each for staff and students. The questionnaires and the slip, which will be separated immediately on receipt, should be **returned by 12.5.98** in the envelope provided. Winners will be announced on 20.5.98.

Many thanks in anticipation of your cooperation.

Yours faithfully,
Professor D. Greenaway

✂ --

BICYCLE PRIZE

If you wish to be entered for the draw, please fill in the details below and tear off this slip. Enclose the slip with your completed questionnaire in the envelope provided and return it through the internal mail. The slip will be separated from the questionnaire immediately on receipt. All personal details will remain absolutely confidential.

Name ....

Department ....

Contact telephone number ....

Please tear off and return with the questionnaire

Approaching respondents for an interview

It is helpful, if possible, to send potential respondents a letter first, including the same kinds of points that would be in a covering letter for a postal questionnaire. Here the letter is functioning as a kind of letter of introduction. Then, when contacting the person by telephone or in person, we can refer back to the letter. We should not assume that respondents will remember the detailed contents of the letter or even having received it – for someone else in the household may have opened it and not mentioned it. The point is, it serves as an introduction and shows our good faith in wishing to elicit informed and willing cooperation.

If calling in person, we will obviously want to look respectable, and not be mistaken for a salesperson or evangelist. We should carry identification with a photograph, and an official letter explaining who we are and giving a contact address and telephone number for verification. As with a covering letter, we need to explain the purposes of the research, how the findings will be used, whether any summary report will be available, how the respondent was chosen, and our guarantees of confidentiality.

One awkward problem is when one member of a household acts as a gate-keeper and tries to refuse participation on behalf of another ('My wife won't want to take part in your survey'). We should do our best, politely, to try to speak to the potential respondent in person.

Piloting

Piloting is essential, but is often skimped and hurried. In our experience sponsors rarely allow for it; they want you to get on with the survey and produce the results.

A pilot survey is a dummy run of the survey proper, in which we aim to test all the key aspects of the survey, including access to respondents, design of the research instrument, and gathering the data. The pilot survey may be preceded by one or more **pretests**, in which we investigate particular aspects of our survey, such as a specific set of questions we consider problematic. The pretests and the pilot survey are all part of the overall process of piloting.

Textbooks on surveys often propose an elaborate and costly programme of pretests, followed by a large-scale pilot survey. It is an ideal impossible to live up to in most research carried out on a limited budget by a solo researcher or a small research team. The answer is not to despair, but to focus on the essentials. We suggest the following guidelines:

- Try to get it right first time. A pilot survey should be as good as you can make it. Piloting enables us to refine our survey, not to transform a hopeless mess into a perfect instrument. Perfection is not attainable anyway.

- Quality is more important than quantity. Small-scale but intensive piloting is far better than large-scale crude piloting.
- Imaginative use of small-scale pretests is very productive. It enables us to get detailed comments and suggestions about how to improve our research instrument.
- Make the pilot survey as similar as possible to the survey proper. In principle, we should be testing the effectiveness of all aspects of the research design.
- Using your judgement about the target population, choose a representative range of respondents for the piloting. Relying on friends or colleagues will not be representative of the target population. Ambiguous, sensitive or offensive questions may not be picked up.

In the piloting process, we need to be attuned to the signs that warn us that something is wrong – as set out in Boxes 5.4 and 5.5.

Box 5.4   Warning signs in pilot self-completion questionnaires

Giving several answers to a question where only one was required This means we need to make our instructions clearer – for example, *please ✓ one only*.

Giving one answer to a question where several were possible Again, the instructions need to be clarified – for example, *please ✓ all that apply*.

Failure to answer the question This may mean that the question is awkward or offensive. Alternatively, something may have gone wrong with our question skips.

Open questions are left blank If hardly anyone answers them, do they have any value?

A question asking respondents to rank items is not completed properly Ranking is a complex task. We should simplify it, usually by reducing the number of items to be ranked.

Respondents write comments in the margins This is a straightforward sign that something is amiss.

The questionnaire takes a long time to complete Even if people do not complain, this is a clear warning. Participants in a pilot survey may be more generous with their time than respondents to the survey proper will be.

Almost everyone gives the same answer This is a warning sign of possible social desirability effects.

Box 5.5 Warning signs in pilot interviews

The interviewer has to clarify or expand on a question Presumably the question is unclear, and needs to be reworded.

The interviewer has to apologize for a question This is an extreme form of the first point. In our experience of being interviewed, it is common in hired hand research. We should never have to apologize for a question.

Interviewees appear reluctant or embarrassed Something clearly is wrong. Some questions may be more sensitive than we realized, or perhaps our self-presentation is unintentionally inhibiting.

The interviews are significantly longer than expected The simple remedy is to cut the number of questions, and perhaps to reduce the amount of probing.

The interviews are significantly shorter than expected This is a warning that rapport may not have been achieved, that respondents have doubts about the research, or that question probes are not operating properly.

There are items where respondents want to say more than we expected This is a sign that these items are salient to the respondent. We should consider asking more questions about them, perhaps with deeper probes.

Respondents have difficulty with response categories We may need to use show cards.

Interviewers have difficulty with instructions Interviewers have problems too. Instructions, especially question skips, are often hard to follow.

Distribution and return of questionnaires

If we are sending questionnaires through the post, or through the internal mail of an organization, we need to make sure that they reach the right people. First, we need up to date addresses. Second, we must make it easy for respondents to return their questionnaire to us. If they are to use the post, then it is desirable to supply them with a stamped addressed envelope, which appears less impersonal than a business reply envelope. In some cases, it may be more convenient for respondents to use the internal mail of their organization, provided it is efficient and provided that respondents are confident it is secure.

Sometimes, questionnaires are handed out personally by an intermediary – for example, by a teacher in a classroom or a receptionist in a waiting area. Relying on intermediaries is, however, very dangerous. Unless they have been fully briefed, and unless we can be quite confident that they will do as instructed, it will probably not turn out well. Good intentions are not enough. Intermediaries may not be fully aware of the nature and purposes of the research, nor are they necessarily knowledgeable about the research process. Sometimes they may go too far, implying that participation is required and refusal not an option. They may give inaccurate instructions, or put an inappropriate gloss on the purposes of the research. In other cases, intermediaries may not pursue the matter at all vigorously, but will simply leave questionnaires lying around for people to complete if they feel inclined. Few will do so.

Self-completion questionnaires are often used in audience research in theatres and like venues. A common problem is that the respondent is given no instructions whatever about where to return the questionnaire. People may be reluctant to leave it behind on their seat. So we see people leaving the theatre at the end of the performance, clutching a questionnaire while vainly looking for the box to put it in or an official to hand it to. Most of these questionnaires finish their life in a litter bin or the gutter. The fault lies with the researchers, for having given no thought to how the questionnaires are to be returned.

Key summary points

- Collecting the data yourself has key advantages.
- Commissioned research requires negotiating the aims of the research as well as the details.
- Respondents need to be persuaded of the value of the research and of their own contribution to it.
- Piloting is essential to successful design.

Points for reflection

- Have you done all you can to encourage respondents to participate?
- Have you dealt with the problems of gatekeepers and intermediaries?
- Have you incorporated all the lessons from your piloting?

Further reading

To pursue these questions in more depth, we suggest that the best way is to read about how researchers have tackled them in their own work. Devine and Heath (1999) provide a good starting point in their *Sociological Research Methods in Context*. Some of the articles in Hammond's (1964) classic collection, *Sociologists at Work*, deal with researchers adapting survey methods to particular settings and problems (see especially the chapters by Lipset, Coleman and Davis).

6 Designing the questions: what, when, where, why, how much and how often?

Key elements in this chapter

- Asking meaningful questions
- Handling sensitive issues
- Being clear without being patronizing
- Dealing with ambiguity
- Using open-ended questions
- Minimizing social desirability effects
- Designing interview schedules
- Coding

The sociological imagination

Formulating the questions to include in a questionnaire or interview sched-ule, designing the layout of questionnaires and planning the sequence of questions: all these lie at the heart of survey work and are one of its most enjoyable aspects. There are technicalities to be taken into account and pit-falls to be avoided, as we explain. But the technicalities stem from something more fundamental, the sociological imagination.

Professional sociologists do not have a monopoly on the sociological imagination. It is grounded in social life – above all, in the lives of our respondents. We use our sociological imagination to try to identify the links between public issues and private concerns, between the great issues of our society such as poverty and social exclusion, disability, job insecurity, and the personal experiences of people engaged with them. We ground our imagination by preliminary work such as reading about the topic, talking to people, observing them, piloting our questions and so on.

Question design calls our sociological imagination into play in a number of ways. We need to frame questions that are meaningful, sensitive, precise, searching, and salient to our respondents. We need to construct the questions in such a way that respondents will want to answer them as fully and truthfully as they can.

Understanding what matters to respondents

Surveys are often criticized for being driven entirely by the interests of the researcher. How do we know that what interests us also interests our respondents? This is the problem of salience. Respondents' helpful cooperation does not necessarily show that we have engaged with their real concerns.

Box 6.1   Gauging salience

Open-ended questions
We examine the significance of open-ended questions later in this chapter. For the moment, we simply say that two of the most productive questions the Survey Unit has asked of first-year undergraduate students at the University of Nottingham, UK, are the following:

> What would you say you have most liked about being an undergraduate student at the University of Nottingham?

and

> What would you say you have most disliked about being an undergraduate student at the University of Nottingham?

Ranking questions
These are closed versions of the open-ended questions given above. We present our respondents with a list of alternatives, and ask them to choose a small number that are the most important to them. Sometimes we ask respondents to rank their selection in order of importance. This technique

---

can be revealing, though it will be very cumbersome if a ranking is required and the list is long. It can also seem somewhat artificial.

Direct questions on salience
We present respondents with a list, asking them to indicate for each item how important it is to them. This approach is blunt, but can be effective.

One very common approach is through a **Likert scale**, thus:

	Strongly agree	Agree	Neutral	Disagree	Strongly disagree
Catering on campus is excellent					
Halls of residence are well equipped					

and so on.

An alternative way of presenting the response categories is like this:

Strongly agree 1 2 3 4 5 Strongly disagree

For each item, respondents are asked to put a ring round the appropriate number.

We suggest later (page 112) that in most cases it is desirable to have an odd numbered scale, normally with five categories, so that there is a middle category. This middle category may be labelled 'neutral', or 'uncertain', or 'neither agree nor disagree'.

Recognizing differences between respondents

An essential reason for doing a survey is to draw comparisons between respondents. If they all thought and acted alike there would clearly be no point in a survey, since we could simply take one case and generalize from it. Variations between respondents can cause technical difficulties, as we illustrate through the *Travel Survey*, but they are what make a survey worthwhile. In our experience, making false or dubious assumptions about respondents is one of the most common problems to be overcome.

Box 6.2   Avoiding unjustified presuppositions and false assumptions

Assumptions and presuppositions are similar but not quite the same.

False assumptions
By an 'assumption', we mean something that is taken for granted. All arguments are built on assumptions, but assumptions can be false.

For example, in a postal questionnaire sent to a sample of Church of England clergymen (this was before the church ordained women priests), Aldridge asked respondents the following question:

Is the fundamentalist approach to the Bible valid today?
☐ Yes
☐ No
☐ Uncertain

A very significant minority of respondents objected to this question, on the grounds that the term 'fundamentalist' was not only ambiguous but offensive. Aldridge had falsely assumed that the term was clear and neutral!

Another example known to us is a questionnaire on cremation and burial, which was delivered by post without even a covering letter and which caused distress to many respondents, not least to people who had been recently bereaved. The researchers presumably assumed, falsely, that the topic was not particularly sensitive, and that it could be treated as an unproblematic area of academic enquiry.

Unwarranted presuppositions
By a *presupposition*, we mean taking the existence of something for granted. The standard philosophical example of this is the question: *Is the present King of France bald?* The point is, of course, that since France is a republic there is no King of France. It is not true that the present king is bald, but nor is it false. In order to ask fruitful questions in our surveys, we need to know what there is and what there isn't in the social world in question. Which of the following posts exist at the University of Nottingham, UK?

Deputy Pro-Vice-Chancellor
Director of Finance
Dean of the Medical School
Proctor

Answer: the second and third exist, the first and last do not. A well-placed member of the university would know this and could have told you if you had asked. Finding out *what exists out there* is a vital component of all social research. We can enquire about the King of France's hair, or the Proctor's policy on student discipline, only after we have established that these beings actually exist.

In seeking to eliminate false assumptions and unwarranted presuppositions there are no easy answers and no simple tactics. We are at the heart of the sociological imagination. Knowing about the social and organizational context is critically important, and piloting plays a key role. Here is one possibility:

Consulting key informants
We have to be clear what we are doing here. Oppenheim (1992: 62–3) warns us against relying on 'experts'. If our questions are sloppy and ill thought-through, it would not take an expert to tell us so, and the expert probably would not waste her or his precious time trying to rescue us from disaster. No 'expert' knows everything. Experts in survey design can help us with technicalities, as Oppenheim says, but they cannot do our thinking for us.

Instead of relying on experts, we should think in terms of making use of key informants. By this we mean people who can help in alerting us to false assumptions and unwarranted presuppositions. They can also warn us about problems in the use of language.

Using unambiguous language sensitively

Obviously, we want questions that are meaningful, clear, unambiguous, sensitive and revealing. Given the variation between respondents, this is not so easy. There are well-known and not so well-known differences in language use depending on social factors such as age, region, and social class.

An issue that has to be dealt with is the social standing of different usages. In contemporary British usage, supposedly 'correct' usages include these:

- the midday meal is *lunch*, not *dinner*
- the room in which the family gathers (if it does!) is the *sitting room*, not the *living room* or the *lounge*
- a *magazine* should never be called a *book*
- the *loo* or *lavatory* is not a *toilet*

Many people are highly sensitive to these variations in usage, regarding some of them as impolite, vulgar, or incorrect. How do we avoid ambiguity without patronizing our respondents or 'correcting' their use of English? Some answers are given in Box 6.3.

Box 6.3   Tactics for dealing with ambiguous or unclear terms

Avoidance
The most commonly used terms for a midday meal are *lunch* or *dinner*, and for an evening meal *dinner*, *supper*, or *tea*. One tactic is to use alternatives such as *midday meal*, *main evening meal*, or *main meal of the day*.

Glossing
Another possibility is to gloss the term, that is, to give a brief explanation of what we mean by it. Here are two interview questions [asked only of those respondents who think their soul will live on after death] taken from the Religion and Politics Survey, 1996, conducted by Princeton Survey Research Associates and accessible on the American Religious Data Archive: http://www.arda.tm

> Do you think there is a heaven, where people who have led good lives are eternally rewarded?
>   Yes (Believe in heaven)
>   No (Don't believe in heaven)
>   Don't know/Refused (Don't know if believe in heaven)

> Do you think there is a hell, where people who have led bad lives and die without being sorry are eternally damned?
>   Yes (Believe in hell)
>   No (Don't believe in hell)
>   Don't know/Refused (Don't know if believe in hell)

These two questions gloss the meaning of heaven and hell. After all, other meanings are common in western culture. For example, some people believe that hell does not entail *eternal* damnation, others that *damnation* not only sounds spiteful but also fails to convey the desolation of being cut off from God.

   Glossing involves an imposition of a meaning. Hence, it is desirable to convey that we are simply saying what *we mean* by the term, not *what the term means*. We do not want to give the impression that we are instructing our respondents in Standard English. Our glossary to this book provides an example. We use **questionnaire** exclusively to refer to a form completed by the respondent; other writers use it inclusively to cover interview schedules as well. We are not claiming that our usage is correct or better, but are simply glossing our use of the term to deal with the ambiguity.

Clarification
This is a form of glossing in which we explicitly clarify potential ambiguity. Here is an example from the *Travel Survey*:

On occasions when you travel to the campus by car, where do you park?
   Not applicable
   In the Science City area
   In the central area (including Highfields House, West Drive and Education)
   On the periphery (including Halls, History and the Sports Centre)

In this case, the location in our categories of Highfields House and the other examples is explicitly clarified. We are in effect glossing what we mean by *the central area* and *the periphery*.

Giving examples

In a Survey Unit questionnaire sent to Pre-Registration House Officers in England – people in their final year of basic medical training – respondents were asked about specific formal educational sessions, and then were asked:

Have any other formal educational meetings been arranged (for example, lectures, journal club, X-ray meetings, etc.)?

Giving examples is far more friendly than issuing instructions, but carries the danger of suggesting some answers while possibly distracting attention from others. It is best used when we know that the examples either cover all the main possibilities or send an unambiguous message about what we have in mind. (Incidentally, the question breaks a rule we were taught at school: you do not say 'etc.' if you have already said 'for example'. However, we think that being clear and helpful is more important than being formally 'correct'. On the other hand, many respondents will be shocked to see misspellings, so it is important to check spelling carefully, running a spellcheck program if possible.)

Indirectly eliminating unwanted meanings

This is sometimes possible, though perhaps risky. It depends on respondents picking up cues from the context. Consider the following example:

Over the past seven days, have you bought any of the following?
Please tick all that apply.
   A comic paper
   A newspaper
   A magazine
   A book

In this example, *book* and *magazine* are listed separately, with *magazine* appearing before *book*. The researcher expects the reader to infer from this that *book* is used exclusively of *magazine*.

The role of open-ended questions

Some books warn against using open-ended questions at all in surveys, while others say that open-ended questions should be kept to a strict minimum. Why is this? Three main reasons are given.

1 Open-ended questions are more difficult to answer, because respondents or interviewees are called upon to think through (or think up) their answer from scratch, without help from the researcher. This is particularly problematic with questionnaires, since writing an answer requires more time and effort than giving it verbally. If respondents suspect that the reason for open-ended questions is that the researcher has not taken the trouble to think about response categories, this may well affect the response rate and the quality of responses.
2 The responses to open-ended questions are more difficult to code, unlike closed questions, where the response categories are pre-coded.
3 The responses to open-ended questions are harder to analyse. Partly, this is because of coding problems. In addition, a number of respondents will simply skip over open-ended questions. Open-ended questions typically have a higher rate of non-response than closed questions do.

Despite these real difficulties, open-ended questions can play an important part in survey work, both in questionnaires and interviews. They can be used for a number of purposes.

To introduce variety

Questionnaires and interviews which rely on a very small number of types of question and response – a Yes/No/Don't Know format, for example – may be straightforward, but are also likely to be seen as tedious. One way of introducing variety is through the careful use of open-ended questions.

To tap salience

As discussed above (Box 6.1), open-ended questions can be very useful in helping us to assess the salience of an issue to a respondent.

To show a humanistic approach

Surveys are sometimes thought to be inevitably mundane, boring and insensitive. By using open-ended questions as well as closed ones, we are able to send a clear signal that we approach our research in a humanistic spirit. Our respondents are *informants*, with their own *individual* points of view, which they are quite capable of expressing *in their own words*.

To acknowledge that researchers are not omniscient

In some cases, we have so little idea of what answers might be forthcoming, or the possibilities are so vast, that it is simply not possible to provide respondents with a sensible list of the main alternatives. In the *Travel Survey*, people who cycle to work were asked the open-ended question:

> How do you think facilities for cyclists could be improved?

Members of the Survey Unit are not cyclists themselves, and could not easily anticipate what the answers from cyclists would be.

To generate quotations

A few well-chosen quotations from our respondents can convey the flavour of responses far better than any other rhetorical device. We are delivering our promise to give people a voice. If our survey is being undertaken on behalf of a sponsor, direct quotation from respondents – who may be customers – can have an immediate impact. There will be good news as well as bad. First, the good news, from postgraduate students:

> What would you say you have most liked about being a postgraduate student at the University of Nottingham?
> 'High quality – the experienced teachers, good courses.'
> 'My lovely friends from all around the world, UK, Taiwan, Turkey, Germany, Greece, Spain, Denmark . . .'
> 'The safe and beautiful campus.'

The bad news:

> What would you say you have most disliked about being a postgraduate student at the University of Nottingham?
> 'Catering is grossly over-priced, especially sandwiches/hot drinks. The overall feel is of a monopolized market.'
> 'Lack of proper union facilities, emphasis on halls to exclusion of post-graduates.'

Used judiciously, direct quotations can bring home to readers the salient issues for respondents – an important aspect of the writing of a research report, which is covered in chapter nine.

Occasionally, an open-ended question can produce an unexpected response which can set the researcher thinking more deeply about the issue. A startling example is the following, from a programme of interviews in Islington, London, in 1968 (Abercrombie *et al.* 1970):

> Do you believe in God?
> 'Yes.'

Do you believe in a God who can change the course of events on earth?'
'No, just the ordinary one.'

This is the only survey question we know of that has given rise to a poem:
Donald Davie's 'Ordinary God' (Davie 1988).

Box 6.4   Making the best use of open-ended questions

Use them sparingly
Open-ended questions require more time and effort on the part of the respondent, particularly in self-completion questionnaires. They are also more difficult to code. As Oppenheim warns (1992: 113), open-ended questions 'are often easy to ask, difficult to answer, and still more difficult to analyse'.

Do not begin with them
It is usually desirable to begin with closed questions, so that the respondent is drawn into the study and rapport is established before the more difficult open-ended format is introduced.

Use them to probe the respondents' view of salient issues
In the survey of postgraduates cited above, two open-ended questions were used to tap into students' best and worst experiences of the university.

Allow an appropriate space for the response
As a general guide, we suggest a space equivalent to three or four lines. Any less, and respondents may conclude that their opinions are not really being taken seriously. Any more, and respondents may feel intimidated or annoyed that an unreasonable effort is being required of them.

Tackling the social desirability problem

A major challenge for all overt forms of social research is the social desirability problem. Respondents tend to give socially approved answers to our questions, to over-report their virtuous actions and under-report their vices, and to engage in socially approved behaviour when they know we are observing them.

The problem of social desirability has a number of dimensions. Respondents may be trying to do one or more of the following things:

- being helpful and cooperative to the researcher by giving the answer they think the researcher wants;
- giving answers that appear to show that they are cultivated people, morally decent, and good citizens;
- demonstrating that they are rational by giving answers that are logical and consistent.

Box 6.5 Tactics for dealing with social desirability effects

- Be specific, asking neither about hypothetical behaviour (what would you do if?), nor about regular behaviour (how often do you?), but about a specific time period (what did you do in the last seven days?).
- Ask indirect questions instead of addressing a sensitive issue head-on.
- Avoid leading questions.
- Make clear – for example in a covering letter – that our research is scientific and ethically neutral.
- Consider using self-completion questionnaires that are completely anonymous and that do not involve personal interaction with a researcher.

Questions about respondents' knowledge

Surveys frequently include questions which tap a respondent's knowledge about a given issue – food hygiene, say, or the effects of smoking on health. This is not the same as asking people for their opinions. In a democratic society, a range of opinion is to be expected, but lack of knowledge equates to ignorance, which is socially undesirable. If respondents feel that they are facing some kind of test designed to expose their ignorance, they may be unwilling to participate. In any case, science is always advancing, so we can never be sure we have the complete truth about these questions, and the line between knowledge and opinion is often less clear than we may like to think.

One way of dealing with the potentially intimidating character of knowledge questions is to present them as questions about respondents' opinions. Phrases such as 'in your opinion', 'in your view' and 'from your own experience' may be used to signal this. We can also provide respondents with a 'Don't know' category.

Avoiding overlapping categories

Very often, we ask respondents to indicate where they fall in a particular range. This can help to soften questions that might otherwise be too sensitive, such as asking about the respondent's age or level of income. Take this example:

Please state your age last birthday:
Under 20
20–30
30–40
40–50
50–60
Over 60

The problem here, obvious once mentioned, is that a respondent aged 30 falls into two categories, namely 20–30 and 30–40. The same problem applies to respondents aged 40 and 50. The categories overlap. The response categories need to be reformulated. For example:

Please state your age last birthday:
Under 20
20–29
30–39
40–49
50–59
60 and over

Asking about age

Presenting respondents with a set of categories, as above, is one common way in which we can minimize people's sensitivities about age. Instead of asking them exactly how old they are, we ask them to indicate into which age range they fall. For many purposes, this will be all we need. If, however, we need to know respondents' age more precisely, there are some technical problems to overcome.

Consider a child aged 5 years 9 months. How many years old is he? Most respondents will say 5 years, but some, a significant minority, will round the age up to 6. This is a problem when asking about the age of children, but it applies to adults too.

One possibility is to ask respondents to state their age in years and months. This may work reasonably well when asking about young children, though even here there is a small technical problem, in that respondents may round to the nearest month. In any case, we often do not need such precision, and adults typically do not think in these terms about their own age.

Another possibility is to ask for date of birth. This is very precise, but can sound excessively bureaucratic and official. A more common solution to avoid the ambiguity is to ask people for their 'age last birthday'.

Avoiding double-barrelled questions

A double-barrelled (or worse, multiple-barrelled) question is one where more than one question is being asked at the same time. For example: 'Do you own a camcorder or video recorder?' is asking about two separate items. A more subtle example is: 'How often are you in contact with your parents?' – here, two people are involved, and the respondents' relations with them may be very different.

One tactic for detecting this problem is to look for the tell-tale words 'and' and 'or', and the use of the slash, as in cinema/theatre.

In general, the problem of double-barrelled questions is more likely to occur in informal interviews than in structured interviews and self-completion questionnaires. The good news is that such questions are also less of a problem in an informal interview, since any difficulty they cause can easily be repaired. Even so, they are better avoided. Consider the following question:

Do you know if your employer has an equal opportunities policy?

If a respondent says 'Yes', we are right to infer that, unless they are being facetious, they mean that the employer does have such a policy. If they are being facetious, their 'Yes' may mean 'Yes I know the answer, but I'm not going to tell you what it is until you ask the question properly'.

So much for facetiousness. What, then, if the respondent replies 'No'? Here there is a serious doubt: does the respondent mean he does not know, or is he telling us that his employer does not have an equal opportunities policy?

In conversation, phrases such as 'do you know if?' are used to allow room for people not to know the answer to a question without any implication that they are ignorant and *should* know. In social research, even in informal interviews, we should find other ways of making it easy for respondents to say that they don't know.

Avoiding negatives, double-negatives and worse

Suppose you are opposed to the policy that students should contribute to their university tuition fees. What is your response to the following question?

Tuition fees should not be abolished
Strongly agree   Agree   Neutral   Disagree   Strongly disagree

Working out your own position on a negative statement such as this can be perplexing. It is a particularly acute problem for people who disagree with the negative; in this example, they do not agree that tuition fees should not be abolished – a double negative. It is far simpler to present respondents with a positive statement, such as:

Tuition fees should be abolished
    Strongly agree   Agree   Neutral   Disagree   Strongly disagree

The main things that go wrong in designing questions, and how to prevent them

Questionnaires that are too long

We should resist the temptation to ask questions out of idle curiosity. Other things being equal, the longer a questionnaire is the lower the response rate will be. The *Travel Survey* is quite short, with a total of 23 questions for staff and 21 for students – and even here, the maximum number of questions any respondent has to answer is only 19. As well as being as concise as possible, the questionnaire needs to be laid out in such a way that it *looks* manageable.

The same point applies to interviews, which should not be prolonged unnecessarily. In arranging an interview, it is normal to provide respondents with an estimate of how long it is expected to take. Common examples are: around three-quarters of an hour; no more than an hour; between an hour and an hour and a half. It is necessary to provide such estimates so that respondents can set aside enough time for them. But do we need to provide a similar estimate for a self-completion questionnaire? Should we say things like: 'this questionnaire will take around ten minutes to complete'? If we do, we need to make sure that our estimate is accurate, or our false reassurance will be counterproductive. In any case, whatever we say, our respondents will judge for themselves whether or not the questionnaire looks worth their time and trouble. On balance, therefore, we think it is normally better to avoid such promises.

Ranking questions that are too complicated

Ranking questions appear to offer an excellent means for gauging the relative salience of items to the individual respondent. It appears very attractive to offer respondents a list of items, asking them to rank them according to their importance. Surely this will yield a rich body of data for analysis?

Suppose we wish to ask a sample of postgraduate students from other countries about their orientation to their studies in Britain. We might decide to ask a question such as the following:

Students tend to have priorities in what they hope to gain from postgraduate study. Judging by what you feel at the moment, please rank the following factors in order of importance to you, putting a 1 next to the factor which is most important and so on down to 9 for the factor which is least important.

To be able to cultivate a wide range of interests
To experience a different culture
To interact with different kinds of people
To develop intellectually
To acquire knowledge and skills to base your career on
To have a full social life
To make new friendships
To develop your sporting abilities
To develop your language skills

What could possibly go wrong with this? Hard experience suggests that a lot can, and probably will:

- Many respondents will not rank all nine items. Instead, they will rank a few – perhaps three of four – and leave the rest blank.
- Some respondents will want to have tied items, and it is very hard to stop them. For example, they may decide that 'to interact with different kinds of people' and 'to develop intellectually' rank equal second. How will you analyse their response?
- Some respondents will not treat it as a ranking exercise. Instead, they will place an × or a √ against the items that matter to them, leaving all the rest blank.
- Some respondents will write in 'all of them'.

There are two ways of dealing with the problems of ranking.

One possibility is to simplify the task. In the example above, it would be more straightforward to ask respondents to put a √ (a tick or a check mark) against the three items that are most important to them. Even so, they would have a long list of complex items to contend with. As another possibility, we could produce a much shorter list – three items, say – and invite respondents to rank them 1, 2, 3. We recommend that five is the maximum number of items that respondents be asked to rank.

Alternatively, we can change the ranking into a rating. The Survey Unit presented the items as follows:

Students tend to have priorities in what they hope to gain from postgraduate study. Judging by what you feel at the moment, please rate how important the following are to you.

	Very important	Fairly important	Not important
To be able to cultivate a wide range of interests			
To experience a different culture			

. . . and so on.

Lack of variety

A very common failing in questionnaire design is to adopt the same format for all or most of the responses. Often, this takes the form of a long series of statements to each of which the response categories are: strongly agree – agree – neutral – disagree – strongly disagree. The layout of such question-naires may be neat and tidy, but they run the risk of being tedious to complete. A bored respondent is seldom a good informant.

Vague questions about frequency of actions

It is very common, in all types of social survey, to gather information about periodical actions. We want to know how often respondents do things. For example, how often do they go to the theatre? We might envisage the following:

> Do you go to the theatre?
> Often   Sometimes   Rarely   Never

But what does this tell us? Suppose a respondent goes to the theatre roughly once a week. Is that often, or sometimes? If they go once a month, is that often, sometimes or rarely? The problem is, of course, that different respon-dents will interpret the categories differently, so we shall have only the vaguest idea of the frequency of attendance among our respondents.

Because the response categories are vague, the danger of social desirabil-ity effects is particularly acute. Going to the theatre is a relatively high-status activity, suggesting an active interest in the arts and the intellectual life. Over-reporting may be a problem. In the case of more socially dubious activities – going to the dogs, perhaps? – under-reporting is more likely.

One way of dealing with periodical behaviour is to offer more specific categories of response, such as:

> How often on average do you go to the theatre?
> More than once   Once a week   Once a month   Once a year   Never
> a week

A difficulty with this is that the response categories, though commonsensi-cal, are not exhaustive. What about someone who goes to the theatre on average every other week – that is, twice a month or six times a year? We have no category for her, and for others whose periodicity does not fit into our categories.

Another problem with this approach is that it assumes that the behaviour in question is regular, an assumption which may be false. Some people go to the theatre several times during holiday periods, but not at all at other times. We have introduced the phrase 'on average' into the question, to try to deal with this difficulty, but a difficulty it remains.

Perhaps we should tighten up the response categories. Thus, for example:

How often do you go to the theatre?
| Never | 1–5 times | 6–10 times | 11–20 times | Over 20 times |
| | a year | a year | a year | a year |

The gain in precision has been bought at the cost of extreme artificiality.

A wholly different approach is to ask people about their behaviour over a specified time period. We might ask them how often they have been over the last week, or the last month, or the last year. This has the advantage of being specific. There are, however, a number of problems to be tackled if this approach is adopted.

To start with, there is considerable ambiguity in asking about weeks or months or years. Imagine a respondent filling out a questionnaire on Friday 18 November. What will she or he understand by the phrase, 'over the last week'? Does it mean the period since Sunday 13 November (Sunday being the first day of the Christian week)? Does it mean the period since Monday 14 November (Monday being for many people the first day of the working week)? Or does it mean the seven days since Saturday 12 November? In many cases, researchers probably mean seven days – in which case we need to say so.

If we use the phrase 'over the last month', this might mean the period since the beginning of the month, or the last 30/31 days, or, more roughly, the last four weeks.

As for years, 'over the last year' might mean the period since the beginning of the year, or the last 365/366 days. In some situations, it will not be clear whether the year referred to is the calendar year beginning 1 January or some other year, such as the financial year or the academic year. In the case of 'over the last twelve months', the fact that we might be a few days short of a full year is unlikely to matter – the period is long enough for it to be a trivial issue.

In contrast, asking people what they did 'yesterday' is not ambiguous. It minimizes the problems of memory recall. The longer the time period the greater the opportunity for memory to be coloured by self-image. A short time period therefore helps to combat social desirability effects.

One potential problem with asking about behaviour 'yesterday' is that it may have been an unusual day. A respondent who, say, has two glasses of wine every day may not have had a drink on that particular day for some special and not often to be repeated reason. In some cases this will not matter. If we have a large sample of respondents, and if we are interested in aggregate data rather than in individuals, these variations will be very minor and will probably be cancelled out (another respondent will, unusually for her, have drunk two glasses of wine on a special occasion).

What will matter is if the time period is exceptional for a significant number of respondents. If we interview people on 2 January about their eating and drinking over the last seven days, we have chosen a period which in many societies is a major feast, and not typical of the rest of the year. Unless over-indulgence at Christmas and New Year is the object of our research, we should choose another period. This is an obvious example, but there are many others where we need to be careful: holidays, the holy days of faiths other than our own, and the beginning and end of cycles such as academic terms.

Selecting a sensible and meaningful time frame is not impossible, but requires some thought and often a little research.

The most effective way of asking about periodical actions will vary from case to case. Given that point, Box 6.6 lists some general guidelines, all based on the need to be as specific and unambiguous as possible.

Box 6.6   Asking about periodical actions

- Avoid 'often – sometimes – occasionally – never' and variants on the theme. Such terms are vague, and mean different things to different people.
- Do not ask about 'the last week', ask about 'the last seven days'.
- If asking about a year, be clear what period is meant – for example, 'since 1 January', 'since the start of the academic year', 'over the last twelve months'.
- Keep the time period as short as you sensibly can, to minimize problems of memory recall and social desirability effects.
- Make sure the time period is meaningful, and sensibly matches the periodicity of the behaviour in question.
- Make sure the time frame is not an unusual one – unless that is the point of the research.

Lack of clarity about confidentiality and anonymity

If we tell respondents that our questionnaire is anonymous, it means that we have no way of identifying which questionnaire belongs to which respondent. This is a strong reassurance, and obviously impossible in interview situations. Even in a self-completion questionnaire, anonymity can be problematic, as discussed on page 23. For example, consider a survey of university staff that asks respondents to state their sex, their rank, and their academic department. Clearly, the researchers could more confidently guarantee anonymity to a male lecturer in a large engineering department than it could to a female professor in a small department of economics. Since anonymity is an absolute categorical guarantee, we need to be sure we can genuinely deliver it.

If we offer our respondents confidentiality, we need to be clear what is involved. The researchers, after all, know who has said what. Confidentiality means that we will not disclose this information to anyone else. Guarantees of confidentiality typically involve the following:

- the use of pseudonyms to disguise the names of respondents, places and organizations;
- changing minor and irrelevant details in order to disguise these names;
- keeping the data securely;
- not allowing access to the data to anyone outside the research team;
- destroying the data at the end of the project, or anonymising it and placing it in an archive.

The most frequently raised problems, and our answers

In our experience, there are a number of issues that repeatedly trouble people when designing questions. The issues most commonly raised with us, and our responses to them, are these.

Should I include a middle category?

For example, in asking respondents about their level of agreement or disagreement with a statement, which of the following Likert scales is preferable?

Strongly agree   Agree   Disagree   Strongly disagree

Strongly agree   Agree   Neutral   Disagree   Strongly disagree

Some researchers worry that if they include the middle category it will be too attractive. Respondents will simply duck the question and take the easy way out. Therefore, so the argument runs, it is better to force respondents into giving either a positive or a negative answer.

Against this is the point that respondents may legitimately be neutral. Forcing them into either the pro- or the anti-camp is artificial, and can be extremely annoying to people who are genuinely neutral on an issue.

Another version of this problem arises in the use of **semantic differential** scales, where respondents are asked to rate their views on a bipolar numerical scale, with opposing adjectives at each pole. Here is an example, taken from the Survey Unit's omnibus questionnaires. Students are presented with a series of terms describing the university, and asked to put a ring round the number which comes closest to their own view, thus:

lively	1 2 3 4 5	dull
friendly	1 2 3 4 5	unfriendly

When using such scales, we recommend having either five or seven ratings –
more is too complicated and adds very little.

With an odd number of response categories there is a middle position –
here, response category 3. But if we presented respondents with an even
number of categories, thus:

| lively | 1 2 3 4 5 6 | dull |
| friendly | 1 2 3 4 5 6 | unfriendly |

we would deny them the middle option. This way of approaching the problem is a little less obvious that the earlier example, but even so it is artificial
and potentially annoying.

In short, we recommend that a middle category be provided unless there
are compelling reasons for not doing so. If questionnaires are well designed,
respondents will not give a neutral answer merely because they are bored or
intimidated. If respondents are neutral or indifferent to an item, that is a
worthwhile finding.

Should I include a 'don't know' category?

This is a similar problem with a similar answer. Whenever respondents can
sensibly be thought not to know about an item, or to be uncertain about it,
we should allow them to express their doubt or uncertainty. Suppressing the
possibility of legitimate 'don't knows' and 'uncertains' merely distorts the
social reality, and may be very off-putting to respondents. If a substantial
percentage of our respondents say they don't know about an item, that is not
a problem but a finding.

Should it be sex, or gender?

Among the basic information we gather in a survey, we usually want to
know whether our respondents are male or female. In an interview we do
not need to ask, and it would be absurd to do so. But what about a self-
completion questionnaire? Should we label this variable *sex*, or *gender*?

This is an extremely complex issue. At first sight, the answer is clear-cut:
it should be sex. Until recently, sex was invariably the label used on questionnaires. The distinction drawn by sociologists is between sex as biologi-
cally given (male and female), and gender as socially constructed (masculine
and feminine). But this raises a host of theoretical, philosophical and ideo-
logical issues. Sociologists have become increasingly concerned about the
implication of biological determinism that is frequently read into the term
'sex'. The same holds true of 'race', a term which is now usually placed
inside inverted commas to show that we repudiate all bogus theories of race
and racial superiority, recognizing instead our common humanity. Nowadays we rightly ask about ethnicity, not 'race'. In a similar fashion, rightly

or wrongly, 'sex' is coming to be a suspect term as far as questionnaires are concerned. Some people prefer 'gender', but others dismiss this as misplaced 'political correctness'.

The answer is definitely not to duck the question completely. So much of social life is structured by gendered inequalities between the sexes that to fail to record the sex of our respondents is to capitulate to ignorance.

Fortunately, we can deal with the problem by formulating our question as follows:

Are you:
    Female   Male
     ☐   ☐

Questionnaire layout

As well as framing individual questions that are as accurate, searching and sensitive as we can make them, we also need to ensure that the overall layout of a questionnaire (and the structure of an interview schedule) is clear, coherent and sensitive. A few simple guidelines should help. In Box 6.7, we comment on how we applied these in the *Travel Survey*.

Introduction

A few sentences briefly introducing the questionnaire, including any overall guidance on its completion, are a must. It does not matter if they repeat some of the matters dealt with in the covering letter.

Instructions

As well as any overall guidance on the completion of the questionnaire, we need to make clear to respondents how individual questions are to be answered. In the *Travel Survey*, you will see that we have given instructions such as '*Please √ one box*' or '*Please √ all that apply*'.

Sections

It is often helpful to respondents, particularly if the questionnaire is fairly long, to divide it into sections, each with a brief introduction to set the scene. Our omnibus survey of postgraduate international students contained the following sections:

• *Section A – Before you came*
  In this first section we are interested in your reasons for choosing the University of Nottingham and your particular postgraduate research/course.

- *Section B – Now you are here*
  In this section we are interested in your opinions and experiences of the University as a postgraduate.
- *Section C – Use of the Internet*
  Increasing numbers of students are now using the Internet and the University of Nottingham's Web site for information. In the next few questions we want to ask you about your use of this technology.
- *Section D – Research students only*
  This section is for students registered for MPhil and PhD degrees. If you are studying for any other postgraduate qualifications please go directly to section E.
- *Section E – Background details*
  In this section we ask a few questions about yourself and your degree course/research.

Use of columns

If possible, it is a good idea to divide each sheet of the questionnaire into two columns. This uses the space efficiently: it cuts down on unnecessary blank space, and it prevents questions from straggling across the page. Questions should be numbered vertically down the columns, as in the *Travel Survey*:

like this:	1	4	*not* like this:	1	2
	2	5		3	4
	3	6		5	6

Question numbering

Numbering the questions is essential in order to avoid confusion. Some writers suggest that questions can have subletters (3a, 3b, 3c and so on). Their main reason for this is that it makes the total number of questions seem less than it is. We believe, however, that it is possibly confusing and tends to look fussy, so we recommend that questions are numbered 1, 2, 3 and so on without any sublettering. Where an overall question has a number of particular examples – as in questions 13 and 14 on the *Travel Survey* – there is no need for separate numbering; they can all be presented under the one question.

Sequence of questions

If possible, we begin with relatively straightforward questions that will be easy to answer. These will 'break the ice', building up the respondent's confidence in the survey. More complex and subtle questions are introduced later. If we wish to ask questions about personal matters such as age, sex, ethnicity, income, and marital status, these are normally placed at the end, by which time we hope to have gained the respondent's full confidence. An alternative is to put these questions at the very beginning, which is why they are sometimes known as 'face-sheet data'. Although bureaucratically neat, in that it 'gets them out of the way', we believe that starting this way is potentially off-putting, and we do not recommend it.

Question skips

It is often impossible to devise a questionnaire in such a way that all the questions are appropriate for everyone to answer. We may well need to have filter questions: depending on your answer to a filter question, you either go on to the next question or skip to a later one.

Too many question skips can be extremely confusing, and can make a questionnaire look cluttered. We therefore try to keep the number of filter questions to the absolute minimum, and to be as clear as possible about where we expect respondents to skip to. This is one of the reasons why questions should be numbered.

Filter questions often take the following form. Question 3 asks respondents if they play a musical instrument. If yes, they go on to answer questions 4, 5 and 6, which ask which instruments they play, how often they do so, and how much they enjoy it. If the answer to question 3 is no, then clearly questions 4 to 6 are irrelevant, so we need to instruct respondents: 'If no, please go to question 7'. Too much of this can be confusing, and sometimes rather annoying: if respondents have to keep skipping questions, it may seem as if the questionnaire is not really designed for them at all.

One way to minimize the confusion and potential annoyance is to include the skip within the question. Here is an example from the omnibus survey of international postgraduates:

Have you received any information about postgraduate training courses since you began your degree?

Can't remember	Yes	No
☐	☐	☐
	↓	

Please ✓ all that apply

If yes, who was offering to provide the courses advertised?

Training body outside the University ☐
The University Graduate School ☐
Faculty/Department ☐
Unsure who the provider was ☐
Other (please specify the provider) ☐

Another possibility is to require respondents to skip to a whole new section, as a way of eliminating confusion.

If a questionnaire has more than one or two question skips, it may well be a sign that something is wrong. Probably we are trying to survey too many different groups of people about too many different things. Perhaps we can cut out some of the questions? If not, then perhaps we can send different questionnaires to different groups? For example, the Survey Unit devised two versions of the *Travel Survey* questionnaire, one for students and one for staff. The main questions were exactly the same; all that differed were questions about the respondents' work.

Sending different questionnaires to different categories of respondent can obviously only be done if we can identify in advance the category to which a respondent belongs. What if we cannot do so? One possibility is to abandon the idea that we can conduct the research by self-completion questionnaire, which is simply too inflexible an instrument for our purposes. We should consider interviewing respondents. One advantage of the interview format is that it is the interviewer, not the respondent, who has to do the skipping.

Conclusion

Here we thank our respondents for their cooperation. We may invite them to offer any further comments at the end of the questionnaire or on an additional sheet. We must also remember to let them know or remind them how to return the questionnaire to us. For example:

> Thank you for taking the time to complete this questionnaire. If you would like to make any further comments please attach a piece of paper. Please return the questionnaire in the FREEPOST envelope provided either in the internal or external mail.

Box 6.7   The layout of the *Travel Survey*

The *Travel Survey* illustrates these principles in action. Each survey has its own particular difficulties to be overcome. We have already mentioned, on this page, the problem of designing a questionnaire suitable for both students and staff. In the end, a separate questionnaire was sent to each.

The sequence of questions was straightforward. We began with factual questions about respondents' journey to work, such as the distance from home to work, the time taken and the means of transport used. We then moved to questions which ask respondents for suggestions about how facilities could be improved. These questions require a little more reflection, but they may also appeal to respondents since they give them an opportunity to have an influence on improving the University's provision. Finally, we ask a series of more personal questions. We hope that, having completed the earlier parts of our questionnaire, respondents will have confidence in us and our research. We offer the guarantee that 'under no circumstances will attempts be made to identify individuals'. Even though the questionnaire is anonymous this reassurance is still necessary, particularly so for people in a minority – a woman technician, for example.

If the sequence of questions was easy to decide, a far more troublesome issue was the sheer complexity of many people's journeys to work. People do not necessarily use the same means of transport every day of the week or every week of the year. Some variations follow a regular pattern, others are unpredictable. A car driver may use the bus on Fridays, when her partner has the car to visit his parents. A pedestrian or cyclist may take the bus or a taxi if it is raining heavily. A member of staff may use the car during school term time, in order to drop children off at school; outside school term, the parent may cycle to work. Some people have long and complicated journeys to work: they drive or walk to the railway station in Derby, depending on the weather, catch the train to Nottingham (or Beeston, if that particular train stops there), and then take a bus or a taxi to the university depending on the time and the state of their finances.

The Survey Unit's questions had to be sensitive to all these possibilities, while keeping the questionnaire short and straightforward. Hence, for example, question 3: *What mode of transport do you use most often for the longest stage of your journey to campus?*

We also faced the problem of question skips. We wanted to ask people for their suggestions about how facilities could be improved. However, we did not want to ask car drivers to speculate about the needs of cyclists, or pedestrians to address what they guessed might be the concerns of people using public transport. Instead, we wished to ask people about problems with which they were themselves familiar. Hence the format of questions 8 to 14. We used a combination of visual and verbal signals (the instructions, the shading, and enclosing questions 8 to 14 within a border) to indicate who should answer which questions. The outcome, which appeared to be successful, is deceptively simple – but it took time to get it right.

Designing interview schedules

So far, we have concentrated on the design of self-completion questionnaires. What about interview schedules?

Essentially, the same principles apply. Even though the interview has the advantage that the researcher can explain any unexpected difficulties and try to smooth over any sensitive items, this is no excuse for poor design. As much thought needs to go into an interview schedule as into a self-completion questionnaire. This is true even when the interview is informal and unstructured. The interviewer needs to be become very familiar with the interview schedule or guide, so that the interview can proceed smoothly without the distraction of the interviewer fumbling for the next item.

The principles governing the sequence of items are the same as for self-completion questionnaires. Questions about personal details are usually held back until the end. As with questionnaires, it is helpful to indicate to interviewees any significant changes of topic within the interview. Here is the way in which Saunders (1990) introduced the various sections of his interviews with home owners in the UK:

> I would like to begin by asking a few questions about your past and present housing.
> I'm interested in getting some idea of how you spend your spare time.
> I would now like to ask a few questions about your household's income and outgoings.
> Finally, returning to the theme of your house and home . . .

Among the specific issues arising in the planning and execution of interviews, and not covered by our discussion of self-completion questionnaires, the most important are: using **probes**; using **show cards**, including **prompts**; recording the responses; and responding to interviewees' queries. We deal with each of these in turn.

Probes

Probes may be classified into two types: probes seeking more detailed factual information, and probes designed to encourage respondents to elaborate on their opinions or accounts of their own experience.

In a structured interview, we may need to probe respondents for fuller or more detailed information. In order to decide on what probes to use, we need to know exactly what information we require.

Unless an interview is entirely structured, there are likely to be occasions when we want to draw our interviewees out, asking them not merely for more information but also to expand on their thoughts, feelings and experiences. We do not, however, wish our interview to seem like an interrogation or inquisition.

Box 6.8 gives a list of ways in which we can probe for a fuller response. We list them in order of intrusiveness, with the least intrusive first.

Box 6.8   Some sample probes for eliciting a fuller response

1   An expectant pause.
2   An encouraging sound: 'mmhmm', 'uh-huh'.
3   Repeating part or all of the interviewee's reply: 'So, you switched to sociology after your first year at university?'
4   Summarizing their response. 'So, your reason for switching to sociology was that you were aiming for a career in market research?'
5   Asking for an example: 'Can you give me an example of the problems you had with economics?'
6   Asking for clarification: 'I'm not quite sure I've understood why you were unhappy with economics. Could you tell me a little more?'

It is desirable to make this kind of probe as unthreatening as possible. An expectant pause is often enough. Silences, if they appear in danger of becoming embarrassing, can be filled with 'mmhmm's and 'uh-huh's, perhaps nodding the head to indicate encouragement. Repeating part or all of what the interviewee has said is often very effective in moving the interviewee to elaborate their earlier response.

These ways of probing are typically more effective than bluntly asking for 'more details'. Although it is tempting to probe by asking, 'Is there anything more you would like to say?' or 'Is there anything you would like to add?', these are as much ways of bringing a topic to an end as they are of opening it up. They invite responses such as, 'No, that's about it', or 'I can't think of anything else, no'.

Show cards

We often want to ask a series of questions which have the same response categories. One way of handling this would be to ask: 'Would you say that you are very satisfied, satisfied, neutral, dissatisfied or very dissatisfied with the following?', followed by reading out each item in turn. This can be awkward, because it relies on the respondent's remembering what the response categories were. The longer the list, the greater the problem is likely to be. Respondents may say things like: 'I'm not very satisfied, no.' The problem will be that we do not know whether to record this as 'dissatisfied' or 'very dissatisfied', so we will have to ask, 'Does that mean that you are dissatisfied or very dissatisfied?' The respondent may feel that he is being corrected in some way for having failed to remember what the appropriate response categories were.

This difficulty is avoided by having the response categories written out on a show card, which we hand to the respondent. In this example, the response card is acting as a prompt or reminder to the respondent.

As well as acting as prompts, show cards can be used to present lists of items to respondents, for example asking respondents to indicate which items they possess from a list of consumer goods. Similarly, a list of age bands or income brackets is typically given to respondents on a show card. Show cards are also used to present material to respondents for comment. **Vignettes** are typically presented in this way. Interesting examples of vignettes may be found in Finch and Mason (1993) *Negotiating Family Responsibilities*.

Responding to interviewees' queries

In an interview, it is not uncommon for respondents to raise queries and questions. If these are points of clarification, or reassurance about confidentiality, we should be in a position to reply to them openly and straightforwardly.

In some cases, particularly in less structured interviews, respondents may ask questions about the interviewers' own beliefs and experiences. For example, in his interviews with clergy Aldridge was asked about his own religious beliefs or lack of them. His response was to say that he would be very happy to talk about those issues at the end of the interview, but would like for the moment to concentrate on the interviewee's own beliefs and experiences. Respondents were invariably happy to proceed in that way.

Recording the responses

In structured and semi-structured interviews, the researcher will typically be recording the responses as she goes along. Just as self-completion questionnaires have to be easy for the respondent to complete, so interview schedules have to be clear and straightforward for the interviewer.

Things will be made easier if there is a clear visual distinction between the questions to be asked of the respondent, and instructions to the interviewer about question skips and probes. Very often, the instructions to the interviewer are printed in bold capital letters.

Unstructured interviews will usually be tape recorded, with the interviewees' agreement, whereas there is no point in taping a fully structured interview. What about semi-structured interviews? If there is a large number of open-ended questions, it may be worth recording the interview and transcribing the relevant parts of it. Full transcription is time-consuming: even with a transcription machine, for every hour's worth of recording you should allow five hours for transcription.

Setting up for coding

When designing a questionnaire or schedule, we need to look ahead to the stage at which we will be analysing the data. All but the simplest surveys will call for inputting the data into a computer.

In self-completion questionnaires and structured interview schedules, all or most of the items will be **pre-coded questions**. We decide in advance what all the categories of response will be. In order to simplify and speed up the process of entering data into the computer, it is helpful to have numbers, in clear but unobtrusive typeface, by the side of each of the response categories. The *Travel Survey* shows how this is done. Question 3, for example, looks like this:

3 Which mode of transport do you use most often for the longest stage of your journey to work?

Please ✓ all that apply

Walk	☐ 1
Bicycle	☐ 2
Rail	☐ 3
Bus	☐ 4
Car as driver	☐ 5
Car as passenger	☐ 6
Motorbike as driver	☐ 7
Motorbike as passenger	☐ 8

Even where respondents are presented with an open-ended question, we sometimes precode the responses. This is only possible where we have a reasonably clear idea of what the responses are likely to be. Where we have little idea, or where the range of potential answers is unmanageably large, then precoding is not possible. The open-ended questions on the *Travel Survey* (questions 8, 9, 12, and the last part of 13) were not precoded.

With open-ended questions, the problem of coding can be acute. Respondents express themselves in their own unique way, and we have to classify their responses under a predetermined heading. Where more than one person is involved in coding, consistency is even more difficult to achieve. Consistency is a problem, but the need to use our imagination and insight to interpret respondents' answers is not a problem but essential to the sociological imagination.

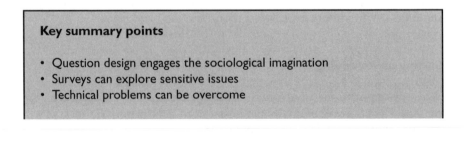

Key summary points

- Question design engages the sociological imagination
- Surveys can explore sensitive issues
- Technical problems can be overcome

> **Points for reflection**
>
> • Would you enjoy completing the questionnaire you have designed?
> • – or taking part in the interview whose schedule you have produced?
> • Are there any questions you are asking merely out of idle curiosity?

Further reading

Oppenheim (1992) *Questionnaire Design, Interviewing and Attitude Measurement* (new edition) is a clear and thorough guide. Devine and Heath (1999) *Sociological Research Methods in Context* examines eight major sociological studies, six of which used a survey as one part of their research strategy.

7) Processing responses

Introduction

The information collected from respondents will normally need to be translated into a digital format in preparation for subsequent analysis by computer, a process that can be termed **response processing**. For large samples and lengthy questionnaires, this translation will involve an extensive amount of routine work, but it also requires some decisions to be taken that will shape the way data analysis can be conducted. In more detail, response processing entails the following elements:

1 The selection of a format for the digital data file within which cases and responses can be recorded, checked, analysed and, if necessary, transformed. The chosen format determines the framework within which elements 2 and 4 will be carried out.

2 The construction of a codebook – a paper or computerized list identifying and labelling the set of variables that the researcher decides to derive from the questions and the responses, together with a sequence of (normally) numeric codes and textual labels that represents all the possible types of response and non-response for each variable.

3 In conjunction with the format of specific questions, the codes chosen in element 2 will determine the level of measurement of each variable: this consideration has major implications for data analysis and is discussed on page 129.

4 Coding – the selection of an appropriate code from the codebook for each case/question and its entry (keyboarding, data input) on to the computer data file: although it is better reserved for this specific process, coding is sometimes used as an equivalent to response processing as a whole.

5 Checking and cleaning the data file.

Some of the methods that can be adopted to handle the response-processing phase deal with particular elements in this list automatically, but it is important for the researcher to appreciate what is happening 'behind the scenes' to prevent unwanted options being adopted by default. The following sections cover each of the five listed items, starting with data input because the scale of this labour-intensive task in medium and large projects can overshadow the other elements in response processing.

Manual, semi-automated and automated data input

The use of a computer to assist response processing and subsequent phases has been presumed principally because manual data analysis is slow, inflexible, limited to basics and error-prone. Very few surveys are now analysed by hand (the exceptions are mainly informal, 'in-house' exercises based on handfuls of respondents and pilot projects where the substantive results may be irrelevant). Computer packages in general are discussed in Chapter 3 but here it is worth noting the variety of possibilities for computer-assisted response processing, starting with the highest levels of automation.

Electronic surveys

Email surveys, web surveys, and surveys conducted using some computer packages (for example, KeyPoint) allow respondents to generate and complete an electronic questionnaire or form on a computer screen. The codebook, codes and levels of measurement are all determined at the point the form is designed so that when a case is returned via email or disk, the responses are already in a digital format ready for analysis. A major attraction of this option to researchers is that the labour of data input is performed by the respondent! A downside is that all respondents require computer access.

Optical Mark Readers (OMR)

An intermediate degree of automation of data entry is possible through the use of OMR equipment. This technique employs custom-printed paper questionnaires in which pen marks made by respondents in pre-designated areas are detected in a scan of the form. The responses that are detected are electronically compiled into a data file. OMR comes in two variants, very expensive dedicated machines that are designed for heavy duty and high throughput (these will be beyond the budgets of most one-off projects), and software applications (such as *Remark OMR,* published by Principia Products) that run on an ordinary desktop computer and read the input from a conventional flatbed scanner linked to the PC. In both cases, the codebook, codes and levels of measurement are all determined at the point the questionnaire is designed.

A relatively simple cost–benefit calculation should indicate whether OMR is an attractive option. In addition to the PC, scanner and software package, the costs need to include printing the custom questionnaires, whose layout is constrained by the requirements of the software. In addition, there are some less obvious costs and limitations. Forms need to be fed into the scanner by hand (time-consuming) or mechanically (an additional expense); open-ended textual responses cannot be dealt with via OMR and have to be filtered out to a different technology; there is always a finite error rate in the scanning process caused by ambiguous respondent marks which have to be resolved by human inspection: the process of scanning OMR forms generally monopolizes the capacity of a desktop computer which cannot be used simultaneously for other purposes.

Specialized data entry software

Computer-assisted telephone interviewing (CATI) and **Computer-assisted personal interviewing** (CAPI) software in which the appropriate questions and prompts appear on an interviewer's screen, dedicated data entry programmes (such as *SPSS Data Entry II*) and many general survey packages offer facilities designed to accompany and assist the manual entry of data via a computer keyboard. The functions available include:

- *Data-entry screens* Some software (particularly the dedicated packages) allow the design of customized computer screen displays for data entry (a choice may be offered between ticking boxes on an on-screen facsimile of the questionnaire/interview schedule, or entry of values into the cells of a spreadsheet where each row represents a case and each column a variable). Supplementary information to assist coding decisions can be supplied to inputters via windows or boxes. Such devices are particularly useful where data input is sub-contracted to hired hands.

- *Constrained entry fields* Software can prevent too few or too many characters being entered for a specific response.
- *Double entry* To ensure input accuracy, each data item is typed twice with the software testing for consistency.
- *Routing* When a response to a question with a filter takes a branch that skips ahead, the software can ensure that the point of entry for inputting the next response automatically jumps ahead also, minimizing input errors.
- *Bounds checking* Numerical limits can be set to ensure that impossible values are not entered as a result of keyboard errors (for instance, in a survey with a target population of employees, attempts to enter a respondent age outside the range 16–65 inclusive could be prohibited).
- *Consistency tests* These ensure that empirically unlikely or inconsistent combinations of characteristics within a case are automatically detected and highlighted (for example, a household which appears to own 20 cars or an individual whose responses to different questions suggest a current status of both employed and unemployed). Such cases could be the result of interviewer mistakes or respondents misunderstanding questions.

Standard office application software

If dedicated software is unavailable, a standard office spreadsheet or database application will provide a more than adequate manual data entry environment that may offer several of the facilities mentioned above. Failing these, a word processor or text editing application will suffice, but some manual way of checking the integrity of the data entered (or a sample of it) should be considered.

Data file formats and data types

If an integrated survey software package has been selected for use in a project, this choice will probably have determined the file format in which the input data is held for analysis and presentation purposes. Such packages tend to employ their own proprietary file formats that are very unlikely to be directly compatible with any of the others. However, many packages allow a range of additional formats to be recognized and imported semi-automatically (and also, to a lesser degree, to be exported).

If data input has to take place before a computer analysis package has been earmarked, the safest strategy is to input the data using a widely recognized file format such as CSV (comma separated value) or TSV (tab separated value). These are very simple text-only files containing a series of data items (the numeric value or series of alphanumeric characters representing each response) separated by a comma or tab character acting as a delimiter (or 'punctuation') between each item. A carriage return character punctuates each respondent's data (each case). A CSV file will consist entirely of printable characters (including spaces) plus carriage returns, and a TSV file printable characters plus tabs and carriage returns. Such files can be created easily in word processors and spreadsheets (exporting in text-only mode) and text editors. A useful option in CSV files is to include as the first 'row' of the file (up to the first carriage return) a list of the names (in quotation marks and separated by commas) of each variable in turn that the data items represent. Any application capable of importing the data file should automatically recognize these as variable names and display them appropriately.

Survey computer packages are capable of recognizing a finite range of data types (that is, variable values). It is obviously crucial to ascertain that the package you select can handle all the types that are relevant to the project in hand. Nearly all packages can handle integers (whole numbers), floating points (decimals), strings (or alphanumerics, with values made up of letters, numbers and spaces) and dates. Some have additional data types for currency and freetext (continuous prose). Packages also differ over matters such as limits on the total number of variables, the maximum and minimum permitted values of integer and floating point variables, the maximum number of decimal places that can be processed, the maximum length of strings, and the characters that can be included within strings (such as punctuation marks and accented characters). A crucial consideration if a questionnaire contains open-ended questions is whether a package can handle lengthy comments. Text handling in several packages is restricted to string variables with a maximum of 255 characters. If this is the case, lengthy responses will either need to be split between several variables, or open-ended comments may have to be directed to an alternative package for analysis.

Constructing the codebook

Before packages for the survey process became available for desktop computers, a codebook listing the sequence of variables with their code assignments had to be written out by hand. Each software package now has its own procedures for eliciting the codebook information which enables it to find every variable in the data file, store the values internally and display the data in a helpful format on screen (providing the names of the variables in a CSV file, as described above, is one way of communicating a vital part of the codebook). Here is a list of items of information that a package might require to construct its database:

- *Variable location* In some types of file format, the computer package needs to know where within the columns of data in the data file the values for a particular variable begin and end.
- *Variable type* As indicated above, survey software may recognize a range of types and require them to be distinguished.
- *Numeric format* The character of numeric variables may need to be further specified – for example, as integer, specific floating (decimal) point format, scientific notation.
- *Variable name/label* Packages may operate with internal reference names that are constrained in length and starting character, but may permit more intelligible variable labels for display purposes.
- *Display formats* It may be possible to control the way the value of a variable is displayed on screen independently of the format in which it is stored within the database.
- *Value labels* These supplement the actual values for display purposes with explanations of the meaning of each kind of response/code.

Although some of this information will be mandatory, other elements such as the labels are normally optional. However, it is usually well worth the time involved to label fully any database file. It is particularly important if there is a team conducting the analysis or reviewing the results in order to prevent misunderstandings over how variables or codes have been constructed. Even solo researchers returning to a file after a long interval can forget the detail of decisions taken months or years previously: a fully labelled database file reduces the researcher's dependence on memory.

Levels of measurement

As Chapter 2 made clear, quantitative analysis of any kind requires the key theoretical concepts in an area of inquiry to be operationalized, that is, to be associated with empirical observations or measurements. In survey research, the question design, the selection of categories to classify the responses and the choice of codes to represent the categories jointly determine the exact manner in which a concept will be transformed into one or more corresponding variables. The choice of categories to classify the responses is fundamental within operationalization because it is the relations that exist between the different categories that sets limits on what sort of measurement will be possible and how sophisticated any statistical analysis of the resulting data will be. Four types of relations, or **levels of measurement**, are conventionally distinguished. They are presented below in ascending order of the sophistication of measurement that can be conducted.

Nominal level

Where the set of categories for a variable possesses no intrinsic order or scale, classification rather than measurement proper applies. Consider, as an illustration, question 20 on the *Travel Survey* questionnaire. There is no intrinsic order for the different working areas within the University. 'Libraries' could have been listed first and coded '1' with the Arts Faculty listed last and given code '10' without anything being upset. Alphabetical orderings of categories are conventional, not intrinsic, orders, so '1' is merely being assigned here as a convenient numerical label (the categories could have been assigned any set of numeric or non-numeric codes as long as each was different – starting at 1 and counting up is simply a matter of convention). Where codes are arbitrary, they are not numbers in mathematical terms and it is not legitimate to carry out arithmetic operations on them (in the above example, there is no sense in which a case in the Arts Faculty is nine more or less than one in the Libraries). As a result, the types of statistical analysis that are possible on nominal variables are severely restricted.

Ordinal level

In a variable at an ordinal level of measurement, the categories do have an intrinsic order. Consider *Travel Survey* question 14. There is clearly a scale of likelihood of change within the categories so that responses in the 'very likely' categories (coded 1) represent greater likelihood of change in commuting patterns than those in the 'possibly' boxes (coded 2), and the latter stand for greater degrees of likely change than those in the 'unlikely' boxes (coded 3). Ideally, 'very likely' should be coded 3, and 'unlikely' 1, but 1 for 'possibly', 2 for 'unlikely' and 3 for 'very likely' is intuitively wrong. Even though the numbers assigned reflect the ordinal nature of the categories, there are still restrictions on how the codes can be manipulated arithmetically, although a wider range of statistics can be used at the ordinal than at the nominal level of measurement.

Interval level

There are very few variables with interval scales in common use in the social sciences, although temperature measured in Fahrenheit provides a natural science example. A unit of measurement is introduced into the picture that enables the 'interval' or quantitative difference between any two measured cases to be established. Because the bottom of a temperature scale like

Fahrenheit is not anchored in the real world constant, absolute zero, but uses the arbitrary (but convenient) point at which water freezes, it is not legitimate to multiply or divide, only to add and subtract, the difference between temperatures. Thus, if Manchester is 80° F and Montevideo is 40° F, you can say it is 40° F hotter in Manchester, but you cannot say that it is twice as hot.

Ratio level

In the highest level of measurement, the bottom of the scale is grounded in a 'non-arbitrary zero' point and there are fewer restrictions on the ways values can be legitimately transformed. Social scientific examples include age, income and population density. Consider also question 11 on the *Travel Survey*. Each respondent who travels by public transport enters a sum in pounds sterling that becomes the value for that case on that variable. It is legitimate to carry out any basic arithmetic operation on these values, so if one case has a value of £3.50 then it truly represents twice the expenditure of another with a value of £1.75.

To summarize, in nominal variables, classification rather than measurement has taken place (although it is still possible to make some quantitative statements about the distribution of cases between the categories). In ordinal variables (such as those with Likert-type categories), only the positions of cases relative to each other on the variable have been measured. In ratio variables, a number of units have been assigned to each case in a way that establishes their absolute positions on the dimension being measured.

Pre-coding and post-coding

It should be clear from the last section that the value a case or respondent possesses on a variable measured at the ordinal level or above is not strictly speaking a code at all but a non-arbitrary measurement that has to be respected. This is true whether the measurement has been carried out by the respondent themselves, as in question 11 on the *Travel Survey*, or by (or on behalf of) the researcher as, for example, where psychological or clinical tests are administered and a score or measure is extracted by the researcher. Of course, it may be necessary and entirely legitimate to transform the original values in ratio variables by, for instance, converting imperial to metric units or dates to a unit of elapsed time. Variables will frequently also need to be linked and integrated in various ways and this is another respect in which computer survey packages can assist and make the researcher's life a lot simpler.

For nominal and ordinal variables, it is useful to assist data entry by printing the codes to be assigned beside the appropriate categories, choices and options on the questionnaire. This should be done discreetly in a small typeface so that it does not distract respondents. If the responses to a question are finite and all of them can be anticipated in advance (as in the question, 'Which of the following products have you bought in the last month?: Product A, Product B, Product C') then the question can be **pre-coded** – that is, all the codes for each response can be determined and printed on the questionnaire in advance of distribution. In other cases, respondents will return some values that cannot be predicted in advance, or there may be so many possibilities that they cannot be listed. (A question eliciting the titles of recently viewed films would present this problem.) A set of responses that cannot be anticipated must be **post-coded** after data collection. Thus, in the film example above, once the titles have been supplied, it is then possible to code them in any appropriate way, for example, into genres (action films, romances, comedies, and so on). A common question format (see the *Travel Survey*, question 20) is to present a set of pre-coded categories intended to cover the majority of respondents, followed by a residual 'Other', category (which will be post-coded) for a minority of special cases. All open-ended questions, by definition, must be post-coded.

Missing data

A general principle in response processing is to avoid using blanks in the data file to stand for cases/questions where there are no values to enter. This is because it is hard to know whether a blank is a deliberate coding decision or an accidental coding slip. It is better practice to reserve dedicated codes for missing data values, chosen to be distinct from possible substantive values. Conventionally, codes such as '99' and '-1' are used for these purposes and some computer survey packages can include or exclude them from statistical processing according to the user's preference. In some situations, it may be desirable to identify the reasons, where they are known, for data being missing. In an interview-based inquiry, for instance, it could be helpful to use three different codes to distinguish between data that is missing because the question was 'not applicable' for the respondent and 'respondent refusal' or 'question not put'.

Multiple responses

In some question formats, such as question 4 on the *Travel Survey*, a respondent can legitimately 'tick' several different response categories. There are three alternative methods of assigning codes to these multiple response questions. Each method preserves all the information supplied by the respondent and which one is most convenient depends mainly on how the data is going to be analysed.

Multiple dichotomies

The researcher creates several **dichotomous** variables in the codebook, one for each tick box a question contains. Each variable has one of its values (by convention, '1') representing the situation where a respondent has ticked that box, and the other value (by convention, '0') representing the situation where the respondent has not selected the category. For question 3, eight dichotomous variables will be created (Walk, Bicycle, Rail, etc.), one for each tick box. For analysis, the multiple dichotomies usually need to be recombined in some manner into more inclusive variables.

Ordinal choices

Suppose, for illustration, that the respondent can make three selections within the same question. The researcher creates three variables in the codebook, called say *Choice1*, *Choice2* and *Choice3*, representing the first, second and third respondent selections respectively. Each of these variables has a set of values corresponding to all the tick boxes. *Choice1* may or may not represent a first preference depending on the question wording.

Binary coding

Only one variable is created in this solution. Each tick box within a question is given in turn a numerical code in the sequence 1, 2, 4, 8, 16, 32 ... The variable as a whole is assigned a value equivalent to the arithmetic total of all the codes corresponding to ticked boxes. Any total represents a distinct collection of ticked choices: if this system was used in question 4 of the *Travel Survey*, a code 'total' of 14 for the question would mean that the respondent had checked 'Walk', 'Bicycle' and 'Rail' as alternative modes of transport.

Checking and cleaning the data

There are two key points within response processing where checking and cleaning the data is advisable. One is immediately after data collection. Particularly in cases where a postal survey has been carried out and the data entry is being done by hired hands or an agency, it is worth going through the forms before they are passed on, looking for problem cases. These may be ones where key fields lack responses (is it worth processing these cases?) or where there are data input dilemmas – perhaps respondents have made comments which were not catered for, or have provided multiple responses where they were not anticipated, or answers which are simply puzzling. It is best to assess the scale of such problems early on and to resolve them before they can affect the confidence and productivity of any personnel hired to carry out data input and coding.

The second strategic point for checking is when the computer survey package has read all of the data available. A few simple checks here can confirm that there are no serious codebook errors. Does the number of cases the software sees match what you anticipated? A frequency count (see page 139) of some key variables will show whether there are any 'impossible' values in key variables which could not correspond to valid responses.

Key summary points

Unless you are conducting a pilot study or a very small inquiry with a handful of respondents, some form of computer assistance with data input and analysis is essential.

- The computer survey package you have earmarked needs to be able to handle all the variable types that you have employed.
- The data file and coding arrangements should be set up to minimize the possibility that missing data are the result of error at any stage.
- A nominal level of measurement sets a limit on the sophistication of the statistical analyses to which a variable can be subjected.

Points for reflection

- Will the question formats and their coding give you a level of measurement for your key variables appropriate to the kind of analysis you are planning?
- Can your data input arrangements cope with the scale and complexity of the task?
- Do you need to set up checks to ensure accuracy of data input?
- Who will be carrying out the data input work? If it is personnel unfamiliar with the research, the codebook and coding instructions will need to be comprehensive and explicit.

Further reading

Although levels of measurement are dealt with in nearly all survey and statistics texts, response processing gets relatively little coverage. Exceptions are Rose and Sullivan (1996), Chapter 3, de Vaus (1991), Chapter 14, and Bourque and Fielder (1995), section 5.

8 Strategies for analysis

Key elements in this chapter

- Objectives in analysing data
- Description, analysis and context
- Analysing open-ended responses
- Describing single variables
- Standardizing variables
- Estimating population characteristics from sample data
- Cross-tabulation
- Multivariate analysis

Introduction

Stated in broad terms, the main goals in survey analysis are the creation of illuminating accounts, persuasive narratives and plausible explanations, grounded in the survey findings, concerning the social structures, groups, and processes under investigation. The statistical summaries of aggregates and sub-groups and the creation of statistical maps of the inter-relationships between key variables are intermediate steps towards these goals.

Some textbook accounts of survey analysis give an almost exclusive emphasis to statistical description and inference, but the imaginative analysis of survey data necessarily transcends statistical reasoning. Moving between statistics and substance demands skill and intellectual agility, with technical statistical knowledge playing an important but not a directing role because statistical methods are a tool not an end. This chapter gives an appropriate emphasis to statistical analysis, but it refers the reader to some of the many texts that are available for more detailed treatments of statistical topics.

A prime objective in what follows is to assist inexperienced surveyors to avoid the danger of getting trapped in a mass of data and losing the plot, for themselves and for the readers of any report based on the survey. This is more of a danger in descriptive than analytic surveys because in the latter the initial questions which fed into the research design provide a landmark from which analysts should be able to get their bearings. However, the strategy sometimes suggested for analytic surveys of organizing analysis exclusively around the empirical testing of a set of specific propositions carries its own dangers. A narrow focus on particular relationships identified in advance can make analysts unreceptive to novelty and the unexpected within the data. For descriptive surveys, statistical strategies for exploring data in the absence of explicit hypotheses are available (see the further reading section at the end of the chapter).

Dimensions of analysis

There are various ways in which the different aspects of survey analysis can be dissected. The three dimensions identified below are conceived to be potentially present in the analysis of any survey although they may not be equally exploited. Unsurprisingly, the descriptive dimension tends to dominate in primarily descriptive surveys. The analytic and contextual aspects will be more pronounced in analytic surveys, but the art of analysis is to promote the development of all three so that the research potential of a survey is fully realized. Ensuring the survey report gives adequate emphasis to each of these dimensions will facilitate the production of the rounded accounts referred to above.

Descriptive

The analyst needs to provide the audience for the survey with a description of the survey findings using such devices as frequency counts for the main variables, statistical summary measures, graphs and charts, and direct quotation from respondent comments. However, a descriptive tour through a questionnaire or interview schedule, in question order, should be avoided for several reasons. First, the structure of the questionnaire is not normally devised with the presentation of results in mind. Second, in order to construct a narrative of the kind mentioned above, the commentary needs to interweave the descriptive with the analytic and contextual dimensions and not present the descriptive material in a block. Third, such an unselective and unstructured approach will quickly lose readers' interest. Description ordered by themes derived from the contextual dimension is nearly always preferable to a question by question catalogue.

Analytical

The analyst will be seeking (to a greater degree in analytic and to a lesser degree in descriptive surveys) to establish links between different questions/variables/sub-groups, to create measures and indicators out of existing variables to represent theoretical concepts, and to develop statistical models or other frameworks that explain aspects of the data. Cross-tabulation, tests of significance, measures of difference, the apparatus of statistical inference which allows generalization from sample data back to the target population, multivariate analysis, model building and testing procedures, all these serve the analytic dimension.

Contextual

The narrower context is the set of hypotheses or problems that were highlighted in the research design, and possibly the theoretical concepts and frameworks which lie behind them. If a statistical model has been developed from the survey data, it will require re-interpretation in terms of 'real world' social structures and interactions. The analyst will need to relate the empirical findings back to the starting points of the research, and at the same time these starting points can supply the themes which determine what statistical description is retained for the final report and how it is organized. Along the way, the analyst will need to highlight the areas in which there are decisive empirical outcomes and summarize those where the findings are ambiguous or contradictory. There is, in addition, the broader context. In the majority of surveys, both analytical and descriptive, the researcher will be keen to locate the outcomes against the backdrop of the relevant setting. In academic or policy spheres, this may entail an evaluation of the significance of the data for rival approaches or previously published findings. In an institutional setting, the implications of key findings for organizational decision-making or community policy may be relevant.

Analysis of open-ended responses

The remainder of this chapter is concerned with statistical procedures but the responses to open-ended questions require a radically different approach that often necessitates the development of a classificatory scheme, so this topic will be dealt with first.

Open-ended material can be generated in a range of circumstances that determine what kind of analysis is appropriate. At the simplest end of the continuum is the 'Other' space provided after a closed question on a questionnaire or in an interview for cases that belong to categories that could not be anticipated in advance. Normally, the respondent is expected to supply just a word or short phrase and the analysis of such material merely requires new codebook categories to be created for the relevant variable (see Chapter 7). A closed question may, however, be followed by a larger 'space' in which the respondent is invited to expand on or explain a previous response. For example, in the *Travel Survey*, question 13 was a closed question that offered respondents six considerations that could be influencing their use of a car for commuting, with the instruction to tick one of three categories of importance. The open-ended question that followed was, 'If there are any other important considerations for you not mentioned above, please describe them here'. This and similar open questions are effectively an invitation to the respondent to add for themselves further rows to the previous question and then respond to them. The framework of the closed question is still operative for both the respondent and the analyst: the responses will be in parallel to, or in extension of, the previous answers and analysis of the additional material should be straightforward.

The most complex open-ended questions to analyse are those that invite the respondent to make a very general or summary response to a topic with the designer deliberately withholding the context for the way the answers are to be framed. An example is, 'What do you think is the most serious problem facing the current Government?' The respondent could approach this in a variety of ways. It could lead some respondents to consider short-term, party political difficulties, while others might be prompted to think about much more abstract issues such as the loss of community or the decline of the public sphere. In addition to lying at different levels of concreteness/abstraction, the material generated may also require the introduction of conceptual distinctions. Thus, some responses will be based on generally recognized perceptions of the gravity of 'established' social problems, while others will stem from a much more personal and localized sense of political grievance and alienation. If there are no more than two separate dimensions underlying the responses, a classification can probably be developed manually and can be applied by sorting the text of the responses into the categories to which they belong, possibly in a word processor. More complex examples will require the use of a qualitative computer package into which all the response text can be transferred for manipulation and analysis. Among the packages that offer appropriate facilities are *Ethnograph, Nvivo, Nud*ist, HyperRESEARCH* and *Atlas.ti* (all distributed in the UK and North America by Scolari – Sage Publications Software).

Table 8.1   Main mode of travel to work (q3)

		Frequency	Percent	Valid percent	Cumulative percent
Valid	Walk	50	8.5	8.5	8.5
	Bike	67	11.4	11.4	19.9
	Rail	1	.2	.2	20.0
	Bus	63	10.7	10.7	30.7
	Car driver	373	63.3	63.3	94.1
	Car passenger	26	4.4	4.4	98.5
	Motorbike driver	8	1.4	1.4	99.8
	Motorbike passenger	1	.2	.2	100.0
	Total	589	100.0	100.0	

Examining single variables

The statistical analysis of survey data will often involve a minimum of two stages. In the first, the analyst produces a variety of exploratory statistical products (counts, charts, summary measures, tables, tests). Some of these explorations will turn out to be dead ends and will have to be abandoned, others will produce findings which have some interest but which are peripheral or are perhaps too detailed for inclusion in a final report (but which nevertheless contribute a little to an emerging picture of the findings). In a second stage, a carefully chosen selection of the products is made that bear on the central research arguments or on the main contextual themes. These products may need to be modified or re-worked to ensure they are mutually consistent and complement one another. The accompanying interpretative commentary is best written at this later stage. It is inevitable that some of the data analysis will need to be abandoned at stage two: there is no obligation in survey research to 'show all the steps in your working' to the audience.

Even in a survey far along the continuum towards the descriptive pole, some variables can be earmarked as being of central interest. On the basis of the research design, common sense or previous inquiries, some principal candidates for the roles of independent, intervening or dependent variables should present themselves. Establishing the distribution of values on these variables is a useful initial step in analysis. The type and level of sophistication of the analysis is limited in situations where nearly all the cases are located in one value category or are heavily clustered around the high or low end of the value distribution – most statistical analysis depends on the existence of variation in values between cases.

Table 8.1 shows a frequency count generated by the SPSS computer package for the *Travel Survey* responses to question 3 – the main mode of travel to work, which clearly has a nominal level of measurement. A table of this kind is useful provided the variable has a limited number of categories (as a rule of thumb, under 20). The 'Valid Percent' column shows the count net of any missing responses (none with this variable, so it is identical to the 'Percent' column). The 'Cumulative Percent' column, which takes the frequency of cases falling in a category, adds the frequencies falling in all the previous categories and expresses the sum as a percentage of the total number of cases, gives a further indication of the overall shape of the distribution.

The mode by which commuters chose to travel to work is one of the *Travel Survey*'s most important variables. An initial consideration of the numbers in each category (using Table 8.1) shows that car use overshadows all the alternatives. This might lead an analyst operating with a brief concerned with the reduction of car use to decide that a way forward could be to explore whether some current car users had realistic alternative travel modes. For example, was there a substantial sub-group of car users who lived sufficiently close to campus for walking or cycling to be at least feasible? The very uneven distribution of cases on travel mode also rules out some other potential strategies. For example, there are too few examples to permit any very detailed examination of those using motorbikes.

The information in the frequency column of Table 8.1 could be represented equally if not more effectively in a graphic format. A bar chart in which the length of each bar is proportional to the number of cases recorded in that category of the variable is appropriate for nominal level variables like mode of travel. A similar graphical method, the **histogram**, can be used for continuous variables, in which case the order of the categories on the chart axis is necessarily fixed and the width of a bar needs to reflect the class interval if these are unequal (as with age bands 0–16, 17–29, 30–49, 50–64, 65+). Figure 8.1 reproduces an SPSS histogram for the ratio level *daily return fare* variable (*Travel Survey* question 11) measured in pence. This indicates a clear peak of cases with fares between 125 and 150 pence, but a tail of higher fares over three pounds. The few cases under a pound are probably people using a bus to or from work only.

A further possibility for displaying frequency data in a graphical format is the stem and leaf plot. These are equivalents for the frequency table, bar chart or histogram, but they are especially useful if there are too many categories to be displayed conveniently as bars. Stem and leaf plots are combinations of the information in a table of frequencies with an adaptation of the graphical principle from bar charts (the length of the 'branches' corresponds to the number of cases in a particular category or denomination). Figure 8.2 is a stem and leaf plot corresponding to the same data depicted in Figure 8.1. The 'stem' in this case represents 100 pence denominations, a convenient 'large' bundle of the units of measurement of the variable. Each branch corresponds to a 50 pence interval within each pound, 50–99, 100–149, 150–199, 200–250, etc. There is no 00–49 branch because there

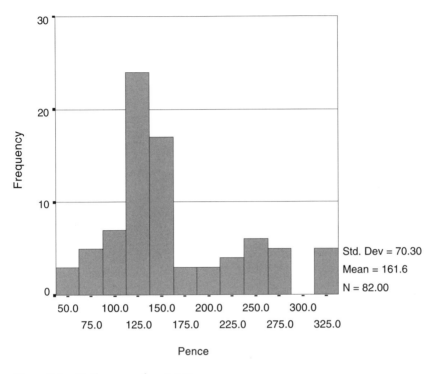

Figure 8.1 Daily return fare (q11)

are no cases with these values. One 'leaf' is placed on the appropriate branch for every recorded case within the interval. Thus the three 6s, five 8s and three 9s that form a branch at zero on the stem stand for the 11 cases of fares between 50 and 99 pence inclusive. Extreme values are often 'trimmed' to reduce the height of the stem, and the bottom of the stem in Figure 8.2 indicates that two leaves and their branches, corresponding to fares of at least £4.20, are not displayed.

This figure conveys a considerable amount of information about *daily return fare* and offers an excellent visualization of the shape made up by the distribution of case values. If the 'typical' fare is reckoned to be roughly £1.30, there are clearly more cases of higher than lower fares. Together with the information from Table 8.1 on choices of transport mode, it seems reasonable to surmise that the relatively small numbers of commuters with lower fares reflect a widespread preference among those having shorter journeys to work to use cycles, go on foot or use a car rather than go by bus. By shifting briefly into the contextual dimension, further possibilities of data exploration become apparent. Given that one of the aims underlying the *Travel Survey* was to estimate the extent to which university staff could be

Q11 Stem-and-Leaf Plot

Frequency Stem & Leaf

```
 11.00 0 . 66688888999
 35.00 1 . 00002222222222222222222333334444444
 13.00 1 . 5555555566778
 11.00 2 . 11122334444
  7.00 2 . 6677888
  5.00 3 . 22233
  2.00 Extremes (> = 420)
```

Stem width: 100.00
Each leaf: 1 case(s)

Figure 8.2   Daily return fare (q11)

induced to reduce their reliance on cars as a means of commuting, the next exploratory step might be to look at the proportions of commuters using different transport modes broken down by the distance between home and work (question 1). With the aid of information from question 4 on the alternative modes that were used at least once a week by respondents, the outlines of a mini-narrative emerge. Among other things, this could examine whether the minority of staff who live close to the campus, but who nevertheless use cars predominantly, was sufficiently large to be worth targeting as a group whose commuting behaviour could be open to influence and change. (As question 14 implies, one option open to the University authorities was the introduction of charges for campus car parking.) Even though more exclusive car users might be found among those living (say) two or more miles away, it is those car users with shorter journeys to work that have more alternative modes of travel open to them.

Measures of central tendency, dispersion, spread and shape

A variety of statistical measures formalize the description of a distribution by selecting a summary aspect. Measures that summarize by reporting a typical or average value are known as measures of **central tendency**, the most common instances of which are the mode, the arithmetic mean and the median. Measures of **dispersion** (such as the range, the standard deviation and the interquartile range) report the degree of variety or spread within a distribution. Finally, measures of **symmetry** (such as skew and kurtosis) provide an indication of the overall shape of a distribution. All these measures are particularly appropriate as aids in examining and comparing distributions of cases on continuous, ratio level, variables, where the amount of numerical detail available could otherwise be overwhelming. A useful bare summary of a frequency distribution can be supplied by offering a measure of central tendency alongside one of dispersion. For example, in the case of the *Travel Survey* variable that featured in Figures 8.1 and 8.2, *daily return fare*, reporting that the mean is 165 pence and the standard deviation is 70.3 pence is much more effective than presenting either one alone because their relative size provides a fairly good snapshot of the overall distribution. Note that the value of the mean differs from that in the stem and leaf plot because some extreme high values were excluded from the plot but included in the calculations in this paragraph. They represent staff who were commuting long distances, probably on a temporary basis while moving jobs or houses, and they arguably distort the overall picture.

A general consideration with measures of both central tendency and dispersion is that a particular statistic may only be used with variables at or above a given level of measurement. As an illustration, the only appropriate summary of central tendency with nominal variables is the mode, whereas ordinal variables can use either the median or the mode, while ratio variables can use both of these as well as the arithmetic mean. Basic statistics and data analysis texts like Healey (1990) and Marsh (1988) provide more detail of the definitions, formulae and applicability of descriptive measures (see the further reading section at the end of the chapter).

Standardizing variables

Standardization is a procedure that assists the task of comparing variables that have been measured in different units. It facilitates the construction of complex indicators out of measures based on different scales and it is a necessary preliminary to the use of various multivariate statistical methods. The calculation of **standardized variables** typically entails subtracting the mean (as a measure of a typical value) from each recorded value and then dividing the remainder by the standard deviation (as a measure of spread). Whatever variables are fed in, the output variables all have a mean of 0 and a standard deviation of 1. The transformed values, known as Z scores, preserve the original scale positions of every case, so no information has been lost.

Statistical inference and sampling error

The descriptive methods discussed above deal adequately with situations of complete enumeration (see page 62), but they do not take account of the consequences of sample selection. Because of variations in the cases making up random samples, it is not safe simply to use sample values to stand directly for target population values. Provided probability sampling has taken place, however, it is possible to use **statistical inference** to estimate the values of population characteristics from the sample data. The outlines of this procedure were presented on pages 76–7. Estimates of any population characteristic can be calculated to a desired level of precision by using a member of the standard error family of statistics that takes into account the size of the sampling error. Thus, the *standard error of the mean* formula is used for calculating the population mean. The result of the calculation is a confidence interval, a range of values surrounding a calculated sample statistic within which the population value will probably fall, with the likelihood of error fixed by the researcher. For example, the mean daily return bus fare in the *Travel Survey*, including the extreme 'outliers', is £1.65. The value of the standard error of the mean statistic for the fares variable is 8.3, giving the lower limit for the range of values that makes up the 95 per cent confidence interval for the mean as £1.48, and the upper limit £1.81. The researcher can assume with a 5 per cent risk of error that the mean fare for the population of all staff will lie somewhere within this range of 33 pence. It is possible to reduce the risk of error to 1 per cent by calculating the 99 per cent interval, but in this case the range of values increases to 44 pence, giving the estimate less precision. See the further reading section at the end of the chapter for texts covering this topic in more detail.

Cross-tabulation

Tabular formats for presenting findings are an important bridge in survey analysis between the descriptive and the analytic dimensions mentioned on pages 136–7. **Cross-tabulations** or contingency tables are so-called because they display each case in a grid of columns and rows in a way that is conditional on at least two of its observed or recorded attributes. By presenting the joint frequency distributions of two or more variables, cross-tabulations combine a great deal of descriptive information with the possibility of making statements about the relationships between the variables concerned. In the familiar, two variable (**bivariate**) cross-tabulation, all the cases from each category of one of the variables are sorted into each of the categories of the other variable. A third variable can be included, in which case one bivariate sub-table is created for every category of the third variable. The third variable may well be a **control variable**, introduced to explore its suspected selective impact on a known independent–dependent relationship.

Although in principle the process can be continued for an indefinite number of variables, there are practical difficulties in displaying and interpreting tables containing more than about four variables simultaneously.

Variables with large numbers of categories present similar problems and adjacent categories need to be collapsed before constructing the final table.

Cross-tabulations are simple but powerful statistical devices and inevitably there are important considerations that must be observed in their construction and presentation.

1 The cells in tables display percentages because it is difficult to make comparisons on the basis of raw numbers: the categories of one of the variables are selected to provide the bases (the denominators) for the percentage calculations.

2 Percentaging is governed by a firm rule – percentage in the direction of the independent (explanatory) variable totals: in other words, a 100 per cent total for each category of the independent variable is created and the frequencies these represent are used in turn as the bases for calculating the cell percentages in the categories of the dependent (response) variable. If there is no clear candidate for explanatory status, then the percentages can be based on either/any variable, but care must then be taken that the table is interpreted in a manner that is consistent with the percentaging.

3 As well as a column (or row) of percentages for each individual category of the independent variable, there needs to be an additional 'All' column (or row), the *marginal totals*, consisting of the total percentages of the independent variable for each category of the dependent variable. This column (or row) of marginal sub-totals should also sum to a 100 per cent.

4 If the independent variable has been given the column position in a cross-tabulation then, as a result of the percentaging rule in point 2, the comparisons will tend to be across the rows, between percentages of the dependent variable in two (or more) categories of the independent variable including the marginal total.

5 Although some texts prefer to place the independent variable in the column and the dependent variable in the row position, this is largely a matter of convenience: from a layout viewpoint, variables with lengthy labels are best located in the row position.

6 Conventionally, the raw numbers (or Ns) for each percentage base are always present in a table so that the original cell frequencies can be calculated by the readers if they wish. The rows and columns which represent numbers need to be clearly labelled to distinguish them from those representing percentages.

7 Tables are numbered in sequence and have conventional titles in the format, '*Table <number>: <Dependent/response variable name> by <independent/explanatory variable name(s)>*': notes and definitions required to understand the table fully are supplied as footnotes linked to specific headings or cells in the table.

8 Because of rounding, some percentage totals may be 99 or 101. Normally

it is best to display the totals as 100 and to explain the rounding error disparities in a footnote in the first table.

9 Tables which have been reproduced from an existing publication always need a precise source: a reference that includes a page and/or table number is essential.

10 Uncluttered tables work best: all superfluous material should be suppressed (unnecessary decimal places, redundant totals): rules (lines) between columns are not essential although they can aid clarity in complex tables.

Table 8.2 shows a cross-tabulation from the *Travel Survey* data from the responses to questions 19 and 22. The direction of percentaging implies that staff group is the independent variable and the number of cars available to the household dependent. (Clearly, how many cars you owned could not be the determinant of which staff category you belong to.) The title reinforces this by naming the dependent variable first – see point 7 in the list of cross-tabulation conventions above.

Table 8.2 reveals only modest percentage differences between the categories of staff. However, there are three interesting features that stand out. First, although the academic and academic related groups are on salary scales that go to higher levels than the other groups, they do not appear to have any greater access to cars. Second, for no obvious reasons a smaller proportion of technical staff is in car-less households than the other groups; and third, more secretarial, clerical and junior administrators are in multi-car owning households than the other groups. Since each staff group contains individuals at very different levels of seniority and stages of their work careers, these findings need to be treated with caution. For example, some members of the secretarial group are young employees who will be in households that possess a car or cars but may not have the use for commuting of vehicles owned by siblings or parents.

There are two simple but important lessons about survey analysis to be learned at this point. The first is that it is hard to make sense of survey findings as an analyst if all you know about the social groups or situations you are investigating is the findings themselves. If this is the case, you need a collaborator or participant to work with you who can provide contextual insights – somebody, for example, who could explain the significance of the different staff groups in the *Travel Survey* and their respective earnings. The second lesson is that it is relatively unusual, especially in descriptive investigations like the *Travel Survey*, for any one finding to be of shattering significance or to stand alone as *the* finding in the project. More commonly, you will be pursuing leads and hunches and hopefully gradually piecing together a developing picture of the slice of the social world that is of interest.

Table 8.2 Cars available to household (q22) by staff group (q19)

	Staff group									
	Academic		Academic-related		Secretarial, clerical, junior admin		Technical		Manual and ancillary	
	N	%	N	%	N	%	N	%	N	%
None	17	10	13	10	18	14	3	4	13	18
One	65	40	60	45	42	32	35	50	40	54
More than one	80	49	59	45	70	54	32	46	21	28
Total N	162	100	132	100	130	100	70	100	74	100

Testing hypotheses and statistical significance

In addition to the technique for estimating population values, discussed on pages 75–7, inferential statistics provides a capacity to establish whether differences observed between sub-groups within a sample on a particular variable (differences, for instance, between means or proportions) are likely to indicate equivalent differences in the population. The same procedures can be adapted to cover situations where the means or proportions to be compared belong to cases that come from different random samples. The central element in the procedures is the testing of a **null hypothesis,** so-called because it always asserts that there is no difference between a sample and a population or between one sample and another. Normally, the researcher hopes to reject the null hypothesis and by so doing to confirm the existence of empirical differences. If it cannot be rejected, the implication is that the evidence is insufficiently strong to infer any real world differences or relationships.

The test of a null hypothesis calculates the probability that the recorded differences in the sample(s) could have occurred entirely by chance on an assumption of no real world relationship between the variables concerned. (Chance, in this context, means simply sampling error, and the tests rely on **sampling distributions** that are theoretical plots of the results from every sample that could possibly be obtained.) If the observed differences are substantial, it will be extremely unlikely that they have occurred by chance. If the observed differences are less substantial, then sampling error becomes more plausible as an explanation and it may not be possible to reject the null hypothesis. By convention, a probability level of ·05 (5 per cent) is generally taken as the minimum threshold of **statistical significance.** In other words, if there is a more than 5 in 100 chance that sampling error could account for the observed difference, the researcher is obliged to accept the null hypothesis. Occasionally, where there is reason to be more stringent, a ·01 (1 per cent) level is also employed. Thus, the outcome of the test of a hypothesis involves two key components, a measure of difference in the form of the calculated value of one member of a large family of test statistics, and a probability statement (usually indicated in summaries of results as $p < ·05$ or $p < ·01$) about the criterion level at which the null hypothesis has been rejected (if the finding is significant) or NS (for not significant) if the finding has a $p > ·05$.

Which sampling distributions are appropriate as the bases for making inferences from different kinds of data is a relatively technical matter about which statistics and data analysis texts give guidance. In general terms, tests which make no, or only easily-satisfied, assumptions about the form of the underlying distribution are known as **non-parametric** and sources describing them can be found at the end of the chapter.

A test of significance commonly employed with bivariate tables containing two nominal variables is the **chi square** test for independence. Symbolized by the Greek character χ (rhyming with 'try' and written as χ^2), it is named after the theoretical distribution it employs. The point of the test is to establish that a case's membership of a particular category on one of the variables has a bearing on which category of the other variable it will be in (and that this effect is distinct from sampling error). The test produces a value that is then compared to a table of chi square distribution values (often reproduced in the back of statistics textbooks). The null hypothesis is rejected if the calculated chi square value is greater than the threshold value in the table for a particular level of significance, which takes into account the number of cells in the table. An above-threshold value for the chi square statistic may also be interpreted as a sign that there is an association between the variables concerned. The chi square value is not, however, proportional to the strength of an association (see the next section).

The same broad logic applies to the **analysis of variance** test of significance (often abbreviated to ANOVA). This is frequently applied to situations where there is a ratio level dependent variable, such as a test score, size or income measure, and a categorical independent variable, such as gender, religious affiliation or occupation (although it can also handle continuous independent variables). In either case, analysis of variance addresses the issue of whether differences between the averages of the dependent variable within the different categories of the independent variable are greater than sampling error would suggest. It does so by comparing the total amount of variation *between* the categories of the independent variable with the total amount *within* categories. The greater the amount by which the between-category variation exceeds the within-category variation, the more likely it is that the null hypothesis can be rejected and an association between independent and dependent variables inferred. Analysis of variance uses the *F ratio* as its test statistic and the *F* distribution as its sampling distribution. There are constraints affecting its application where the numbers in the categories of the independent variable differ greatly.

Statistical texts discuss more fully which test statistics and sampling distributions are appropriate for particular kinds of data and set out in detail the steps in the testing procedures. It is worth emphasizing here, however, two general aspects of testing. Since the logic of calculating statistical significance involves the attempt to discount the effects of sampling error, there is no point in testing the significance of data that is not derived from probability sampling. Secondly, statistical significance is not the same thing as substantive or research significance. It is possible to establish any number of statistically significant results that have no bearing on the objectives of the research (or indeed on the field of inquiry as a whole). The reverse is also possible. A real-world difference or relationship may fail to achieve statistical significance (the sample size may have been too small to permit sampling error to be dismissed). This second point highlights a general limitation of significance tests: outcomes are sensitive to sample size as well as the size of recorded differences.

Measures of association for nominal variables

The calculation and inspection of table percentages is a mainstay of survey analysis in basic surveys. In the case of simple tables, this approach has the advantage of being straightforward from the viewpoint of both production and consumption. However, the comparison of percentages between categories has a number of limitations that are not adequately dealt with by the responses to complexity suggested on pages 144–5 (collapsing categories or examining a series of bivariate sub-tables if there is more than one independent variable). A severe limitation of all the bivariate procedures reviewed so far is that they do not provide a straightforward measure of the strength of the relationship between the variables.

Measures of association address this deficiency. For nominal variables, there are two main families of simple measures of association. The first family is based on the chi square statistic and derives additional measures from it, the most common of which are *phi* (for 2X2 tables, written as φ) and its close relation, *Cramer's V*. The values of both of these (and many other indices of association) take up values between zero (for no association) and 1.00 (for a perfect association). Both are relative indices in the sense that the closer to zero the weaker and the closer to 1.00 the stronger the association. However, neither measure indicates the proportion of the overall variation within a table that is attributable to the association. Both chi square-based measures are normally accompanied by an indication of the outcome of the test of a null hypothesis.

Table 8.3 Staff group (q19) by main mode of commuting (q3)

	Academic	Academic-related	Secretarial clerical, junior administrator	Technical	Manual and ancillary
	%	%	%	%	%
Walk	11	7	8	4	13
Bike	15	8	7	16	8
Bus or rail	8	6	18	7	14
Car (driver/ passenger)	65	77	68	69	61
Motorbike (driver/passenger)	1	2	0	4	4
Total	100	100	100	100	100

The second family, **proportional reduction in error** (PRE) measures, such as *lambda* (written as λ), are based on a comparison between two attempts at prediction. In the first attempt, the value of the dependent variable is predicted in a state of ignorance about the values of the independent variable; in the second, it is based on the values of the independent variable. If there is a sufficient improvement in the accuracy of prediction between the first and the second attempt, an association between the two variables can be inferred. The results of a PRE test are also presented as an index between zero and 1.00, but an important advantage of a PRE index over a chi square-based equivalent is that it has a more intuitively meaningful interpretation. A lambda of .25 is an indication that knowing the values of the independent variable reduces the error factor in predicting dependent values by 25 per cent. As a result of lambda being an asymmetrical measure, results will be different depending on which variable is identified as independent. Under some circumstances, lambda is ultra-conservative and produces results indicating no association when other tests result in positive outcomes.

To see the application of a PRE measure, consider the *Travel Survey* issue of whether there is a relationship between membership of a staff group and main mode of travel to work.

The percentages in Table 8.3 are not easy to interpret. The manual and ancillary group appears slightly less dependent on cars than the others and it contains a larger proportion of walkers and a smaller one of cyclists. There are also slight divergencies from the 'average' among the other groups, but it is difficult to judge whether there is an overall association between the two variables. Here the measures of association can play a valuable role. Table 8.4 reports the results of two measures of association conducted by the SPSS package for the data contained in Table 8.3.

Table 8.4 Main mode of commuting (q3) and staff group (q19) – measures of association

| | | | | Asymptotic standard | | |
		Value	Error[a]	Approx. T[b]	Approx. Sig.
Nominal by nominal	Lambda	Symmetric	.019	.010	1.865	.062
		Staff group dependent	.027	.014	1.865	.062
		Main mode of travel dependent	.000	.000	[c]	[c]
	Goodman and Kruskal tau	Staff group dependent	.015	.005		.006[d]
		Main mode of travel dependent	.016	.007		.003[d]

[a] Not assuming the null hypothesis.
[b] Using the asymptotic standard error assuming the null hypothesis.
[c] Cannot be computed because the asymptotic standard error equals zero.
[d] Based on chi-square approximation

Because lambda can be symmetric or asymmetric, the table shows three results: one for mode of commuting dependent, one for staff group dependent, and 'symmetric' for neither dependent.

The second part of Table 8.4 reports the results for another PRE measure, *Goodman and Kruskal's tau*, which is sensitive to some patterns of association not detected by lambda. There are two rows of results for tau because it only exists in an asymmetric form. As far as lambda is concerned, with main mode of commuting dependent the result is zero association. The picture with tau is effectively similar. The index of association at .015 is very close to zero and there are no grounds on the basis of these results for assuming a relationship between these two variables. Where the measures of association are so close to zero, the existence of statistical significance is irrelevant.

Measures of association for ordinal variables

A consideration that applies to this category is whether the variable concerned is *continuous or collapsed*. The variable containing the score resulting from a series of linked questions employing a Likert scale will be continuous – many score values for a case will be possible. *Spearman's rank order correlation coefficient*, known as *rho* (r_s), is appropriate here (see the next section for more on correlation coefficients). Values vary from zero to 1.00 and have no direct interpretation, though the square of rho, r_s^2, can be interpreted in the same manner as lambda.

If the number of values of an ordinal variable has been reduced via the way the raw scores are processed, or as a result of a subsequent re-coding operation, then *gamma* (G) is a relevant test statistic. Gamma values also lend themselves directly to PRE-type interpretation.

A minor complication that affects measures of association for ordinal variables is that they each treat differently pairs of cases that have the same score/rank on the independent or the dependent variables (or both).

Measures of association for ratio variables – correlation

Association between two ratio level variables (or between pairs within a larger matrix of continuous variables) can be measured by *Pearson's correlation coefficient* (r) that has a similar form to the ordinal coefficient in that it takes up values between zero and ± 1. Coefficients with minus values indicate a negative (inverse) association with values moving in opposite directions – as the values of one variable decrease the values of the other increase. Positive coefficients indicate that as one variable increases (or decreases) in value, the other moves in a similar direction. A zero coefficient and the

Table 8.5 Miles (q1) and time (q2) correlation

		Miles	Time
Miles	Pearson Correlation	1.000	.701**
	Sig. (2-tailed)	.	.000
	N	588	587
Time	Pearson Correlation	.701**	1.000
	Sig. (2-tailed)	.000	.
	N	587	588

** Correlation is significant at the .01 level (2-tailed).

values surrounding it imply no association while values close to 1 approximate to a perfect (positive or negative) association. Values intermediate between zero and 1 do not have a direct interpretation but, as with the ordinal coefficient, squaring the r value produces a statistic that offers greater intelligibility. Called the *coefficient of determination* (r^2), an r^2 of .25 would indicate that 25 per cent of the total variability of the two variables is accounted for by their joint variation and that 75 per cent comes from other (unknown) sources.

Correlation is a symmetrical measure: if variable A is strongly correlated with variable B then necessarily B is with A to the same degree, and there is no facility in basic correlation for stipulating or inferring which is dependent and which independent. It follows from this that evidence of strong correlation coefficients is, in the absence of other analytic or contextual information, never adequate to establish causal connections.

In the case of the *Travel Survey*, it is relatively safe, given the intervals and the number of cases, to convert the responses to questions 1 and 2 from the bands (class intervals) used on the questionnaire into the units of new ratio variables (*miles* and *minutes*) by assuming that all responses lie at the midpoints of the bands. The resulting textual output from the SPSS computer package is in Table 8.5.

The table presents the information twice, once from the 'viewpoint' of each variable though the views are necessarily identical. All variables correlate perfectly with themselves, which accounts for the two cells with coefficients of 1.000. As could be anticipated, the actual *miles–time* correlation of .701 is strong, and its coefficient of determination (not reported in the table but .49) indicates that co-variation accounts for just under half of the total variability. The software automatically conducts a test of significance the outcome of which is significant at the .01 level, suggesting that it is very likely that the association would also hold for the population of all staff.

Because of the mathematically superior information contained within pairs of variables measured at the ratio level, it is possible to go beyond a measure of association and to analyse how a quantitative change in an independent variable is translated into a quantitative change in a dependent variable. The kind of argument used in the PRE measures can be reapplied to this situation. In the absence of any additional information, the best guess (prediction) for the value of a case in the population on a dependent variable (Y) – in *Travel Survey* terms again *minutes* – would be the mean value of all the sample cases on *minutes*. However, if there is an independent variable (X) that has a linear correlation with *minutes*, like *miles*, then knowledge about this additional relationship can be used to improve the accuracy of the prediction. A linear relationship implies that a unit increase or decrease in *miles* will result in the same amount of change in *minutes* across the whole range of values of *miles*.

The scattergram provides an opportunity to graphically plot the linear relationship between these or any two continuous variables. A single straight summary line, the least squares regression line, can be drawn by a computer through the scatter of coordinates that represent the joint distribution of cases. It is so-called because it minimizes the total sum of the squared distances between each coordinate and the line itself. Its slope is a direct measure of the linear relationship between the two variables. Reading along the axis representing the independent variable and taking a vertical line to intercept the regression line gives a prediction of the value of a case on the dependent variable. The existence of a correlation will result in a prediction superior to one based on the mean of all the sample values on the dependent variable.

The graphical plot of regression can be shown to represent an equation of the form

$$Y = a + bX + e$$

where Y is the predicted value of the dependent variable, a is the *intercept*, the hypothetical value of Y for which X is 0, and b is a coefficient reflecting the slope – the effect on Y of a unit change in X. Regression equations being used for prediction also need to incorporate a *residual* error term e that covers the variation that remains unexplained by the linear association between the variables.

Some general points on testing significance and measuring association are:

- hypothesis testing is only applicable and meaningful in respect of data derived from probability samples, but measures of association are relevant more generally (for example where data is the product of complete enumeration);
- where two variables have different levels of measurement it is generally safe to use measures of association appropriate to the lower level;

- redefining or collapsing the categories of nominal variables in order to conduct repeated tests in the hope of finding statistically significant differences is bad practice;
- there are hidden dangers in conducting a series of significance tests on differences between pairs of categories taken from the same independent variable; the risk of mistakenly rejecting a null hypothesis over a series of such tests is higher than the level of significance adopted for the individual tests.

Multivariate analysis

All of the techniques discussed above are primarily designed for analysing associations in a pair of variables at a time. Several of them, including percentaged tables, can be extended to handle a limited number of variables simultaneously. **Multivariate analysis** is a generic name for a large number of different statistical techniques all of which are designed to represent the relationship between families of variables. In order to establish the effects of a control (intervening) variable on an independent/dependent pair, the approach suggested on page 144 was to construct and compare a set of bivariate sub-tables, one for each category of the control variable. Such a procedure is termed **elaboration** and there are three possible outcomes from inspecting the sub-tables (or **partials**).

1 Confirmation of the original relationship: each sub-table reproduces the original relationship essentially unchanged.
2 A spurious or an intervening relationship: the relationship in each of the partial tables is much weaker or disappears completely: this is an indication that the control variable is possibly a determinant of both the original independent and dependent variables. Alternatively, the original independent variable may affect the control variable and this in turn affects the dependent variable. Which of these possibilities applies has to be established by considering the variables and the temporal links involved rather than statistically.
3 An interaction: the original relationship is stronger in some partials than others: this indicates that specific values of the control variable enhance the relationship between the original independent and dependent variable, while others attenuate or suppress it.

Clearly, each outcome has different implications for the direction to be taken in subsequent analysis. The mechanics of elaboration are described in greater detail in, for example, de Vaus (1991), Chapter 12 or Healey (1990), Chapter 17.

While elaboration has the merit of being relatively intuitive, it has limitations. The procedure lacks an intrinsic measure of association; some kinds of interactions between the non-dependent variables may be difficult to detect simply by inspection; where the independent variables have many categories, the number of sub-tables can quickly become unmanageable. It is possible, in principle, to collapse categories, but this will be at the expense of a loss of information, and collapsing categories may be hard to justify with nominal level variables in which each category is fundamentally different from the others. The most effective response to a situation in which an analyst wishes to examine the simultaneous mutual influence of several independent variables on one (or more) dependent variables is to use one of the more advanced multivariate techniques.

Central to most of these types of analysis is the notion of a process in which the investigator attempts to fit a statistical model to empirical data. A simple version of fitting was described in the previous section where prediction based on linear regression between two ratio level variables was under scrutiny. More generally, fitting a model can be understood in terms of a simple equation,

observed data value = value predicted by statistical model + residual term (unexplained variation)

The relationship between a statistical model and a substantive theory raises technical considerations that go beyond the scope of this book. From a practical viewpoint, fitting a statistical model to observed data means producing an effective summary description of the way the values in a set of variables are inter-related. Effective implies 'simple' and 'accounting for a satisfactory degree of variation'. Process is an apt term because there may be a series of models to be tried in succession, and also because fitting any one of them can entail an *iterative* or stepwise procedure in which particular variables are added to or subtracted from consideration in order to improve the degree of fit. (What variables are included or removed is a consideration where both contextual and theoretical considerations are relevant.)

A key statistical model for survey analysis is the **general linear model** (GLM) which underpins some of the most widely used multivariate techniques including both simple linear regression and multiple linear regression. In the case of the latter, the model can be expressed along the lines of an extended version of the equation set out on page 154. On one side of the equation is the population value of the dependent variable to be predicted. The other side is made up of the independent variables included in the model, each one of which is accompanied by a statistical coefficient (or multiplier), plus a residual for the unexplained variation. The equation for two independent variables looks like this (the way in which further variables would be incorporated is self-evident):

$$Y = a + b_1X_1 + b_2X_2 + e$$

This kind of equation does not lend itself to representation in a two-dimensional plot so the notion of slope is no longer appropriate.

The 'b's indicate the standardized regression coefficients (or multipliers) for each of the independent variables in the equation and the use of this symbol reflects the fact that they are also known as *beta coefficients*. Although their precise statistical form varies with the exact multivariate procedure in question, regression coefficients have a standard interpretation. They indicate the amount of change in the dependent variable that results from a single unit change in the particular independent variable with which the coefficient is paired, with the effects of all the other independent variables in the equation suppressed (that is, controlled).

There is no suitable ratio level dependent variable on which to conduct a multiple regression analysis in the *Travel Survey*. However, if sufficient detailed data could be collected, such a technique could come into play to attempt to predict, for example, the distance away from the site of work at which staff choose to reside. Such an equation might feature the following kinds of variable:

$$\text{Distance from home to work} = \text{Cost per mile of return journey} + \text{Journey time} + \text{Number of buses/trains available} + \text{Number of cars available}$$

However, it is very likely that such a model would still leave a good deal of variance in the location of homes unexplained. The comments in response to the open-ended question 13 in the *Travel Survey* made it clear that an important attraction of car use was that it enabled the commuter to do other household tasks alongside getting to work. Dropping children off to school, giving other family members a lift, and picking up shopping are some of the tasks that were mentioned. In analysis terms, the implication of this is that the variable *journey time* which might be thought to capture the superior convenience of a door to door car journey as against the walk from the bus stop or station, may in fact seriously underestimate the flexibility of the car as a mode of commuting in the eyes of its users.

Multiple regression is an extremely powerful and flexible family of techniques and, as is invariably the case, its use comes with a series of preconditions, limitations and restrictions. It is generally necessary with all advanced statistical techniques to anticipate their requirements at the research design stage so that a suitable sample size and variables with appropriate data types are available. The main preconditions and restrictions, together with some ways of handling them, are:

- Predominantly ratio variables: there is scope for converting categorical variables to a series of 'dummy' dichotomous variables which can then be included in regression equations.
- Simple random sampling is presumed though other probability designs may be acceptable.

- A normal distribution of cases on the dependent variable for any value of the independent variables: if this is violated, statistical transformation of the values of the dependent variable may be possible.
- There is a basic assumption that the relationships between all the independent variables and the dependent variable are linear (see page 154). Scattergrams (scatterplots) can give an indication of non-linearity: dealing with it requires the conversion of the data, using a logarithmic transformation, into a format in which linear relations can be detected.
- The regression techniques described above do not cope well with situations in which there is a substantial degree of interaction or correlation between the independent variables to be included within a regression equation: again, this obstacle can be handled by the application of more sophisticated statistical techniques though the cost is greater complexity in interpreting the results.
- The residuals (or standardized residuals) in regression equations need to meet assumptions of independence, linearity, normality of distribution and constant variance: statistics texts discuss the tests available for each of these conditions and the possible antidotes to their violation.
- Exceptional cases (outliers) can distort interpretation leading to the detection of spurious relationships on the one hand and the suppression of real ones on the other: there are techniques for detecting outliers and regression equations can be calculated omitting them in order to evaluate the scale of their impact.
- Predicting the value of a dependent variable beyond the range of values for which there is observed data is not advisable.
- Unless there is a definite temporal or logical order among variables, regression equations indicating high levels of association will still leave the issue of causation open.

Because of the large number of options in conducting regression analysis and because there are multiple statistical criteria for the data to be analysed to satisfy, a detailed guide to applying the procedures should be consulted (see the further reading section at the end of the chapter).

Box 8.1 Further important techniques of data analysis

Partial correlation
An extension of basic correlation techniques that allows the effects of selected independent variables that may affect a bivariate relationship to be controlled. Whereas r_{xy} symbolizes the standard or *zero-order* correlation coefficient between X and Y with no controls, $r_{xy.z}$ (a first order partial correlation coefficient) measures the association between X and Y discounting the effects of Z, while $r_{xy.ab}$ (a second order partial correlation

coefficient) simultaneously discounts two variables, A and B. Partial correlation uses a recursive procedure in which zero order coefficients are fed into a formula to generate first order coefficients, which, if desired, can then be fed back into the same formula to produce second order coefficients, and so on.

Factor analysis
This is often applied at an intermediate stage in the analysis process for either of two main purposes. The first is to reduce large correlation matrices containing many independent variables to much smaller sets of 'hybrid' *factors* which contain elements of all the original variance-predicting variables combined together and weighted in such a way that each explains as much of the variation in the dependent variable(s) as possible. None of the factors that are produced will be correlated at all with each other. One problem with this application is to find a meaningful theoretical interpretation for the hybrid variables that emerge out of the analysis. A second use of factor analysis is to demonstrate from the scores of subjects that the different items included within a measuring instrument such as a pencil and paper test actually tap the same entity or dimension.

Path analysis
A form of *causal modelling*, the most sophisticated level of analysis, which requires an initial set of variables for which the temporal relationships are already established. By means of regression analyses, measures of the associations between all the variables are calculated and tested for significance. Weak linkages can then be ignored and dropped from further consideration. The end result is a graph made up of arrows associated with indexes that measure the precise influence each variable has on the others. Unlike some other multivariate techniques, the links in path models have directionality and are thus one step closer to real world mechanisms and processes.

Log-linear analysis
An approach, based on the GLM model, to explaining associations in categorical data (cross-tabulations that are made up of nominal or ordinal level variables). The technique considers all the variables in the table to be independent and treats the observed frequency in a cell or cells that is to be predicted for the population as a function of all of them. In order to produce an effective and simple model, an iterative procedure based on a goodness of fit test is used to eliminate variables and statistical artefacts that do not contribute to accurate prediction. In *logit* variants, a dichotomous dependent variable is presumed.

Key summary points

- The objective in survey analysis is to construct a coherent picture of a piece of the social world and, if possible, to tell an explanatory story about it: statistical techniques are tools to help you achieve these objectives.
- Survey analysis necessarily involves moving repeatedly between your original research design (and the theoretical ideas it incorporated), the data and the context: exploring hunches, trial and error analysis, dropping unpromising avenues of inquiry, are all legitimate and largely inevitable.
- Do not rely on uncovering a discrete novel or key finding.

Points for reflection

- Will you be hampered in the analysis by a lack of knowledge about the broader context of the inquiry? If so, is there an 'inside' informant or expert collaborator that you could consult?
- It is best to be explicit about research issues that your analysis cannot resolve and generally frank about the limitations of your conclusions.
- If your data is incomplete or inconclusive, can other research fill in the gaps?

Further reading

There are many general textbooks on data analysis and statistics for the social sciences. Some introductory British ones are, Rose and Sullivan (1996) *Introducing Data Analysis for Social Scientists*, second edition, which comes with a dataset on floppy disc; Bryman and Cramer (1990) *Quantitative Data Analysis for Social Scientists*, which contains many worked examples of the analysis of survey data including multiple regression; Fielding and Gilbert (1999) *Understanding Social Statistics*, which is linked to data sets, exercises and a glossary available from a web site. A useful, purely statistical text is Healey (1990) *Statistics: A Tool for Social Research*, second edition, which covers descriptive, inferential and multivariate procedures. Detailed coverage of descriptive statistics can be found in Loether and McTavish (1974) *Descriptive Statistics for Sociologists*.

Marsh (1988) *Exploring Data* is an excellent guide to exploratory methods of data analysis in surveys although it does not cover inferential statistics. An intermediate level treatment of statistical tests commonly used in the social sciences is Siegel and Castellan Jr. (1988) *Non-parametric Statistics for the Behavioural Sciences*. Norusis *Guide to Data Analysis* (various SPSS releases) is helpful for users of the SPSS survey software package (the use of this package is also covered in Rose and Sullivan, Fielding and Gilbert, and Bryman and Cramer). Gilbert (1993b) *Analysing Tabular Data: Loglinear and Logistic Models for Social Researchers* is a useful guide to this increasingly popular technique. Factor analysis and regression are dealt with in Everitt and Dunn (1991) *Applied Multivariate Analysis*, and also in Bryman and Cramer.

9   Presenting your findings

Key elements in this chapter

- Addressing an audience
- Structuring a research report
- Using tables, charts and diagrams
- Writing effectively

Writing for an audience

In 1995, the Economic and Social Research Council published a booklet entitled *Writing for Business*. It contained the following extract from a research team's summary of their work:

> The research will present a structuralist informed challenge to both positivistic and humanistic/post-structuralist approaches to the study of the environmental crisis, and in particular to the neo-classical environmental economics paradigm.
>
> (ESRC 1995: 13)

Far from being a parody, the example is real and typical. What lesson can we draw from it?

To the academic community, the key words in the extract are: 'structuralist', 'positivistic', 'humanist/post-structuralist' and 'neo-classical environmental economics paradigm'. It is not that they are wrong, since these are key theoretical ideas. Academics understand such code words, and know where the researchers are coming from. It is just that, to everybody else, the one arresting phrase is 'the environmental crisis'. The problem is not one of substance, but of communicating to an audience.

The ESRC booklet also gives some of the reactions of business people to research reports. For example:

> If I can't get to the point of a report quickly enough, it goes in the bin.
> (Jan Buckingham, Public Affairs Manager, Allied Domecq plc,
> 1995: 4)

> I simply haven't the time to read everything on the off chance that there's something of interest.
> (Dr Tony White, Head of Corporate Strategy, National Grid plc,
> 1995: 1)

And, more positively but also more poignantly:

> I've got on my desk now a very important piece of research – I think.
> (Sam Porter, Chief Economist, Boots plc, 1995: iv)

Problems in communication tend to lead to mutual recriminations. The researchers may accuse the readers of ignorance and narrow-mindedness: they are only interested in short-term profits, the bottom line. The audience may accuse the researchers of arrogance and hiding behind jargon. Yet we can also see, in the examples above, a recognition that research findings are often very important, if only we could understand them.

It may be helpful to begin by considering what an audience of non-specialists will be looking for in a report of the findings of a social survey. We suggest three basic points:

- Non-specialist readers want to know what the survey found, whether the findings are important, and if so how they can be put to use.
- Non-specialist readers will often expect the researchers to produce not just findings but also recommendations.
- Non-specialist readers are less interested in the methodological details and the complex statistics.

The classic approach to constructing a research report recognizes that these are the readers' basic requirements. Findings and recommendations are highlighted, while methodological complexities are given in appendices for those who are interested or need to know.

Writing for a specialist audience – as in an article for a specialist journal (Box 9.2) – involves giving more attention to reviewing the existing literature, discussing theory and concepts, and providing rich details of methodology and findings.

Characteristics of the classic research report

Overt macrostructure

The overall structure of the classic research report is clear for all readers to see. It will be divided into a number of easily identified chapters or sections. The *Travel Survey* shows one example of this (see Box 9.1).

Box 9.1   *Travel Survey* – macrostructure

Title
Contents page
Key Findings
Section 1:   Background
Section 2:   Staff Survey
Section 3:   Student Survey
Section 4:   Commercial Vehicle and Visitors Census
Section 5:   Open-ended Responses
Summary

Appendix 1:   Definition of commuting modes
Appendix 2:   Staff and student questionnaires
Appendix 3:   Covering letter
Appendix 4:   Commercial and visitors census forms

The *Travel Survey* was a report prepared for a sponsor who wanted hard data to inform rational policies. The structure of the report reflects this. Other situations call for different approaches. Box 9.2 shows a typical structure of a research report in an academic journal.

The rules are not hard and fast, but vary from context to context. The underlying principle of the classic research report remains the same: the macrostructure of the report should be clear and readily identified.

Frequent signposts

To ensure that the macrostructure is clear, the classic research report contains plenty of signposts. Readers are reminded where they are in the argument. We do not want our readers to get lost – hence the signposts.

Box 9.2   A paper in an academic social science journal – macro-structure

Title
Author
Abstract
Keywords
Theoretical introduction and literature review
Research methods
Findings
Conclusions
References
Acknowledgements
Biographical note

Academic writing is full of signposts: 'it was shown in Chapter 2 that . . .', 'it is first necessary to consider . . .', 'I shall argue that . . .'. Signposts can be overdone, and often are; but better too many than not enough.

Threefold structure

Implied in the idea of frequent signposts is a threefold structure. The readers are told where they have been, where they are now and where they are going. People often say a piece of writing should have 'a beginning, a middle and an end'. Or, as the standard advice to teachers has it: you tell them what you're going to tell them, then you tell them, and then you tell them what you told them.

The *Travel Survey* displays this threefold structure. The key findings present essential material in seven bullet points (see Box 9.3). The body of the

---

Box 9.3   The *Travel Survey* – Key findings

- A large proportion of University staff rely exclusively on cars for commuting: they value the flexibility and convenience of the car and may be resistant to changing their existing travel patterns.
- The lengthy travel times for those travelling to work by car reflect the fact that the journey to work can often involve one or more stops en route.
- Staff currently combining car use with alternative modes of travel appear to be more open to changing their travel arrangements.

- The possibility of working from home was considered attractive by a substantial number of staff.
- There was widespread demand for improved cycle facilities, both in numbers of comments and the range of improvements suggested.
- Students mostly walk or cycle and live less than two miles away from the campus.
- Many requests were made for more frequent buses, more direct bus routes and subsidized fares.

report, sections 1 to 5, presents these findings in more detail. The report ends with a summary (Box 9.4). Characteristically, the summary not only repeats the key findings, it also amplifies and adds to them. It also suggests, indirectly, what some of the policy implications of the survey might be. The threefold structure is more than mere repetition.

Box 9.4 *Travel Survey* – **summary**

Staff depend heavily on cars to get to work and many tend to be 'exclusive car users' who appear to have permanent access to a car for commuting. Students mostly walk or bike and live less than two miles away from the campus.

The main attraction of the car for staff and students is its flexibility and convenience. Staff who travel to work by car take longer than those using other modes of transport and the open-ended data suggest that this is because a journey to work often involves one or more stops en route. Dropping children to nursery and school, spouses to work and shopping were some of the tasks done before arriving at the campus. It might be expected for these reasons that exclusive car users will be reluctant to alter their travel patterns. From the survey responses, the most likely influence that might alter the way this groups travels to work is the prospect of more direct bus routes. Although few students use a car to get to the campus, those who do tend to rely on it exclusively and may also be hard to deter from car use.

Staff combining car travel with alternative modes of transport appear more flexible and likely to change. Higher proportions of this group than exclusive car users were 'very likely' to alter their travel patterns for each of the developments we listed in question 14 (subsidized travel cards, more direct bus routes, campus car park charging, improved shower facilities and improved cycle security).

> The option of working from home was popular among staff and is one way campus traffic might be reduced. High proportions of academic, academic-related and secretarial staff find the prospect of working from home 'very attractive'.
>
> Daily bus fares are mostly under £2, the median fare for staff was £1.40, for students it was £1.09. Frequent requests were made from both staff and students who currently use this mode of transport (or would like to), for more frequent buses, more direct buses and subsidized fares.
>
> There was widespread demand, both in numbers and range of suggestions, for improved cycle facilities. In particular, respondents asked for improved storage and security, more and better cycle paths, and facilities for showering.
>
> With respect to the census of commercial traffic, visits to the campus build to a mid-morning peak, slowing down in the late afternoon. The vehicle used is typically a van and will usually make a single delivery on campus most weekdays. The census held in the Social Sciences car park suggests that visitors are often the sole occupants of cars and come to the campus fairly frequently.

Passive voice

The classic research report avoids the personal pronouns 'I' and 'we', nor does it address the reader as 'you'. Instead, extensive use is made of the passive voice, as in this sentence itself. So, instead of 'I interviewed twenty respondents', the researcher says, 'Twenty respondents were interviewed'. One problem with using the passive voice is that we can easily be led into verbiage, so that 'Twenty respondents were interviewed' becomes 'Interviews were carried out with twenty respondents'.

Past tense

Although few writers comment on it, the use of the past tense is a significant feature of the classic research report. The report is retrospective: these *were* the hypotheses, this *was* the research method, the responses *were* these. Only in the final section, if at all, is the writer likely to switch to the present tense: these *are* the conclusions, and further research *is* needed.

Use of tables, figures and diagrams

In the *Travel Survey*, we presented our findings graphically in the form of tables, as for example Table 9.1.

Table 9.1   Regular mode of transport to the campus among students

Mode of transport	N	%
Walk	133	47.2
Bicycle	82	29.1
Car as driver	47	16.7
Bus	13	4.6
Car as passenger	5	1.8
Motorbike as driver	2	.7
Total	282	100

The great advantage of tables is that we can use them to present a wealth of data economically. Readers are able to see all the information, to form their judgements about it and to perform further analysis if they wish.

The problem with tables is that the main points may not come out very clearly. Some readers will not know what to make of a table – how to 'read' it. Tables lack visual impact, even if we use borders, bold type or colour.

Instead of tables, we can use various ways of representing our data to greater effect (see also pages 139–42). These are particularly useful when communicating with a non-specialist audience. Their drawbacks are that they usually involve some simplification of the data, and that readers cannot easily perform their own analysis of the data since they may not have all the information they need. A specialist audience will normally expect this detail – perhaps in an appendix – in addition to the figures and diagrams.

Where we wish to illustrate the proportions in which a variable is divided into its different values, a **pie chart** (also called a pie diagram) is appropriate. In Figure 9.1, the data are taken from Table 9.1 and presented as a pie chart showing how students divide up in terms of how they normally get to the campus. Readers are probably struck immediately by how many (47 per cent) walk to campus. The eye might then be drawn to the second largest proportion, the 29 per cent who cycle to work. Readers might also notice how few use a motorbike (1 per cent), or travel as a car passenger (2 per cent) or even by bus (5 per cent).

Pie charts are less effective when there are many segments, or when some segments are very small. In Figure 9.1, travelling by motorbike (1 per cent) is a sliver and travelling as a car passenger (2 per cent) is only a tiny segment. If the pie chart is small, the slivers may disappear altogether. One possibility is to combine them into an 'other' category, which preserves the visual impact, though at the cost of a loss of information.

Where we are reporting on frequencies, **bar charts** and **histograms** are a straightforward way of presenting basic information clearly. Figure 9.2, drawn from the *Survey Unit*'s survey of international students, presents data

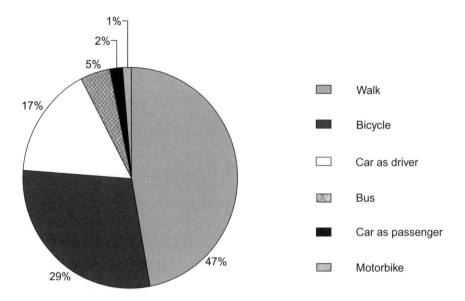

Figure 9.1 Regular mode of transport to the campus among students

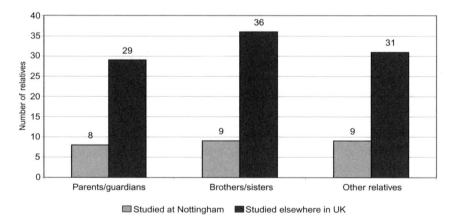

Figure 9.2 International students with relatives who studied in the UK

on the number of international students whose relatives have themselves studied in the UK. The data are broken down into different categories of relative. In addition, the figure shows the numbers who studied at Nottingham compared to other UK universities.

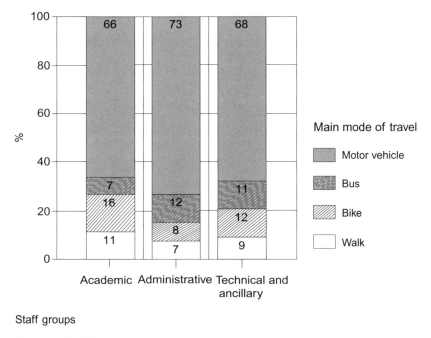

Staff groups

Academic N=162
Administrative N=263
Technical and ancillary N=146

Figure 9.3   Mode of travel by main staff group

A way of bringing out the differences in the joint distribution of two variables is by a stacked bar chart. Figure 9.3, based on *Travel Survey* data, shows vividly the general dependence by all staff groups on commuting by car, but it also highlights the more widespread use of both bicycles and walking by academics compared to administrators. In this particular figure, visual comparisons of the relative importance of different modes of travel have been assisted by making the total number of observations for each group form the basis of the percentages for each stack.

Line graphs are useful for presenting data on social trends. Figure 9.4, based on invented data, shows comparative trends in car ownership among staff and students. The line graph can be effective in highlighting overall trends, differences between categories, and peaks and troughs in the data.

In all these ways of presenting data, we should provide readers with sufficient information to enable them to interpret the data correctly. Depending on the nature of the data and the format chosen, such tables and figures should have:

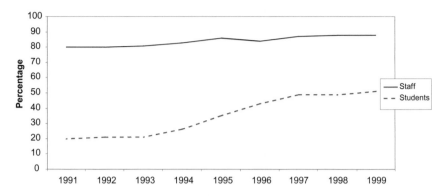

Figure 9.4   Staff and student car ownership 1991–99

- a title;
- appropriate labelling of the columns and rows of a table;
- appropriate labelling of the x (horizontal) axis and y (vertical) axis of a diagram (if one variable is treated as an independent variable, it is conventionally assigned to the horizontal axis);
- a legend identifying the segments of a pie chart, or the elements of a bar chart, or the lines on a line diagram;
- an indication of the units of measurement (for example, litres, miles, thousands of £s);
- an indication of the number of cases involved;
- an acknowledgement of the source of the data if we have not generated the data ourselves.

Reporting on the research methods

In all social science research we need to make our research methods transparent to the reader. Science thrives on criticism, and criticism thrives on information. Readers should be given all the information they need in order to evaluate our research and to replicate it if they wish.

How we provide the information varies according to the audience for our research report. In the case of an article in an academic journal, we will be expected (see Box 9.2) to include a section giving details of our research methods. An academic thesis will typically have a large section or whole chapter devoted to methodology. A research report (see Box 9.1) normally presents this material in one or more appendices.

The details we need to provide cover three aspects of our research methods. Depending on the context, we should consider including the following.

1 Information about the sample:
- sample size
- sampling frame
- sampling procedure
- demographic characteristics of the sample
- response rate
- discussion of the representativeness of the sample

2 Information about our research instruments:
- reasons for choosing the method of data collection
- piloting procedures
- reliability and validity
- a copy of the questionnaires or interview schedules
- who gathered the data
- when and where the data were gathered
- techniques of data analysis

3 Discussion of research ethics:
- access to respondents and documents
- consent and overtness/covertness of research
- confidentiality or anonymity
- information and feedback provided to respondents

Advantages of the classic approach

1 *Clarity* The emphasis on signposting, the use of tables and charts, and all the repetition and redundancy should mean that information is conveyed clearly and unambiguously.
2 *Ease of scanning* The prominence of the macrostructure makes it easy for a reader to scan the report quickly in order to grasp the key points. Beginning with key findings – in business circles, an 'executive summary' – enables the reader to get the gist in minutes, even seconds. The time-pressed corporate executives cited at the beginning of this chapter expect to find an executive summary. The key findings of the *Travel Survey*, the outcome of weeks of work by the Survey Unit, are condensed into precisely one hundred and fifty words.
3 *Scientific register* Avoiding personal pronouns in favour of the passive voice contributes to the flavour of a scientific report. Impersonality conveys objectivity. The structure of the report is geared to transmitting information as efficiently as possible. Other considerations – a racy style,

an intriguing narrative, witty asides – would be seen as irrelevant distractions from scientific reporting of hard data.

4 *Credibility* The impersonal scientific register is designed to elicit credibility. Conforming to the canons of the orthodox research report is less risky than departing from them. In commissioned research, this is what the sponsor is paying us for.

Disadvantages of the classic approach

One of the main challenges to the survey method, discussed in Chapter 1, page 12, is the humanistic critique. Social surveys are said to be a misguided attempt to imitate the natural sciences. Consistent with this critique, the style and structure of the classic research report are seen as pseudo-scientific. They betray, it is alleged, the anti-humanistic nature of the survey method. This basic challenge is reflected in a number of specific points:

1 *Dullness* Clarity, repetition and redundancy, impersonality, information transfer: the report may be at best dry and at worst boring, but in either case it will be devoid of human interest.
2 *No surprises* A strength of the classic research report, its standardization, can also be a weakness. Predictability can be represented as a problem: our findings were predictable, and no survey was needed to report the obvious. Our readers knew all this already.
3 *Misrepresentation of the research process* The classic research report provides an untrue account of the research process. It implies that the researchers began by formulating a clear and distinct set of hypotheses, which they then tested using a carefully designed set of instruments. Findings are then written up efficiently and objectively. It is not a natural history of the research process but an idealized artificial construct that misleads readers about the nature of scientific enquiry.

Far from being a murder mystery where the *dénouement* is saved up to the very end, the classic research report announces its findings in a summary at the very beginning. The report suppresses narrative: we are not to tell the story of the research process as it unfolds, but to reconstruct it in an idealized form. Readers inevitably lose all sense of the thrill of the chase.

Anyone who has ever engaged in research knows that this idealized account is fiction. Research is messy, chaotic and unpredictable. Hypotheses are typically vague ideas. Clarity emerges during the research process rather than preceding it.

We can consider the problem of misrepresentation by examining the distinction between writing and writing up.

Writing up

In the classic research report, and in the natural sciences, preparation of the report is customarily referred to as 'writing up'. Similarly, the final year of a research degree such as an MPhil or PhD is officially described as 'the writing up stage'. What does this phrase imply? Writing up is:

- the final stage of the research process;
- a retrospective account in the past tense;
- an objective report of findings;
- in which clarity is the only relevant literary value;
- in which rewriting is mainly polishing: removing grammatical and spelling mistakes and other infelicities;
- and in which the emphasis is on organization: which bits to put where, and which bits to leave out.

Writing

As we have seen, the classic research report does not aim to give a natural history of the actual research process. Instead, it is a selective and idealized construct conforming to a set of conventions whose goal is to transmit information efficiently.

The idea that writing begins only after all the other stages of the research process have been completed is untrue to the way in which many projects are actually prepared.

Leaving the writing to the writing up stage is to ignore the point, emphasized by Alasuutari (1995), that writing is a tool of thinking. It is not that we have clear and distinct ideas in our minds which we then commit to paper. Rewriting is more than polishing and elimination of spelling and grammatical mistakes, more too than adding literary embellishments. Our ideas are refined in and by the processes of writing and rewriting.

In most research projects the writing process begins early on. This is true of social surveys as well as field work and ethnography. Survey researchers often keep a field diary, in which they record their impressions, their ideas and their intellectual puzzles. Alternatively, they may use a tape recorder. Noting our ideas and impressions is obviously invaluable at the pretesting and piloting stages, but it is also useful in the main survey. For example, one of the things interviewers would do well to record is their impressions of the way respondents reacted to key questions. This can be particularly important in identifying the issues that are salient to respondents, and in exploring the nuances of responses to complex or sensitive issues. Here again is an advantage of gathering the data yourself, since all such insights, however penetrating, are lost in hired hand research.

We should also consider the question of grammatical tense. As already noted, the classic research report is written in the past tense. In contrast, field work in sociology and social/cultural anthropology is typically written in the present tense – the so-called 'ethnographic present'. Readers are told that the Azande *believe* this, that the Dinka *do* that, and that among the Dogon this *is* the kinship system. The ethnographic present tends to stimulate the reader's interest, while the past tense tends to slacken it.

It is not necessarily a question of choosing one tense or the other. Referring to the summary of the *Travel Survey* shows that past and present tenses are used side by side. There is an underlying pattern:

- The present tense is used to present facts about staff and students, for example: 'Staff who travel to work by car take longer than those using other modes of transport and the open-ended data suggest that this is because a journey to work often involves one or more stops en route'.
- The past tense is used to report responses, for example: 'There was widespread demand, both in numbers and range of suggestions, for improved cycle facilities'.
- The present tense is used for recommendations, for example: 'The option of working from home was popular among staff and is one way campus traffic might be reduced'.

The past tense distances the researchers from the respondents' opinions: this is what they told us, and we are just the messenger. If we use the present tense, it may convey some sense, however subtly, that we endorse their point of view. Consider the difference between:

'There was widespread demand, both in numbers and range of suggestions, for improved cycle facilities'

and

'There is widespread demand, both in numbers and range of suggestions, for improved cycle facilities'.

The first statement is agnostic about the cycle facilities and the demand, while the second statement may carry a hint that this demand is not going to be satisfied unless the inadequate facilities are improved.

Writing up *and* writing

It is usually possible to combine the virtues of writing and writing up. The classic, written up research report does not have to be badly written. Even if the summary of key findings/executive summary and the formal conclusions are present in staccato, bullet point fashion, there is likely to be scope for a different approach in the main body of the report. Whereas the typical article in an academic journal demands to be read from beginning to end, one advantage of the research report format is that it makes it easy to read the report in many different ways and sequences. Its apparently rigid structure is actually very flexible.

It is no disparagement to sociology and the other social sciences to say that they are, among other things, forms of literature. As such, they should be a pleasure both to read and to write.

Key summary points

- Survey reports are structured accounts.
- Readers should be supplied with comprehensive information.
- Reports can and should be well written.

Points for reflection

- How will the audience read the report?
- How can its impact be increased?

Further reading

Gilbert's edited collection (1993a) *Researching Social Life* contains a useful final chapter by Gilbert himself on writing about social research. Alasuutari (1995) *Researching Culture* is insightful about the writing process, even though he is sceptical about survey research. To sharpen one's style, Evans (2000) *Essential English for Journalists, Editors and Writers* and Cutts (1996) *The Plain English Guide* offer excellent advice.

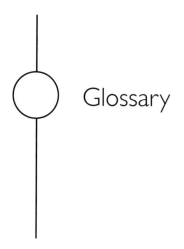

Glossary

Accuracy: In the context of sampling, how closely an estimate from a **sample** coincides with the **population parameter** it seeks to predict.

Alphanumeric (field): A variable in a computer database that contains a combination of number, letter and punctuation characters.

Analysis of variance (ANOVA): A form of statistical analysis often used where there is a metric dependent variable and categorical independent variables.

Anonymity: Respondents have anonymity if it is not possible for anyone, not even the researchers, to trace their responses back to them; *see also* **confidentiality**.

Bar chart: The graphical representation of a nominal or ordinal variable in which each bar represents a category: the length of each bar is proportional to the observed frequency in that category.

Bivariate: Any statistical device or measure that deals with two variables at a time.

Case: The ultimate unit in relation to which information in a survey is collected (for example, an individual or a household).

Case study: A research strategy involving the close examination of one social setting, in contrast to the **survey** and the **experiment**.

Categorical (discrete) variable: One in which the categories are logically separate and form no natural order (for example, the categories of a *religious faith* variable might be *Hindu, Muslim, Greek Orthodox*, etc): see also **continuous variable**.

Census: A survey, often of human individuals or households, in which the objective is **complete enumeration** of the target population.

Central tendency: Statistical measures (such as the mode or arithmetic mean) that summarize a **frequency distribution** in terms of its typical value.

Chi square (χ^2): A test of **statistical significance** often employed with two nominal variables to demonstrate that they are not independent.

Closed questions: Questions in which respondents are given a set of alternative responses from which to choose; also called closed-ended or fixed-alternative questions.

Cluster sample: A **multi-stage** sample design in which the target population is divided up into a large number of areas containing clusters of geographically adjacent cases: the final stage selects a number of these clusters at random either collecting data from every case or a large proportion of the cases within the chosen clusters.

Codebook: A list, now usually computerized, of the variables that will be derived from a **questionnaire** or **interview schedule** with information including the codes assigned to different responses and their labels.

Coding: The selection of an appropriate code for a response to a question in a **questionnaire** or **interview schedule** and its entry into a computer **data file** (sometimes used to refer to all aspects of processing responses).

Complete enumeration: A survey which does not employ any selection procedure but which attempts to collect data from every case in the **target population**.

Computer-assisted personal interview (CAPI): A laptop computer and specialized software is used to generate on screen the questions and prompts for the interviewer and to record the responses by the interviewee.

Computer-assisted telephone interview (CATI): Similar to **CAPI** but using a desktop computer to conduct telephone interviews.

Confidence interval: An estimate of any population characteristic from sample data in the form of a band of values that reflects the researcher's acceptance of a fixed likelihood of error; thus, in a 95 per cent confidence interval for a population mean, there will be a 5 per cent chance that the actual population mean falls outside the band.

Confidentiality: Responses are confidential if the researchers guarantee that no one outside the research team will be able to trace any response back to the respondent who gave it; *see also* **anonymity**.

Contingency table: See **cross-tabulation**.

Continuous variable: A **metric** variable, such as weight or time, made up of many ordered categories, in which the unit of measurement is in principle infinitely divisible: see also **categorical variable**.

Control group: In an experimental design, a group which, unlike the experimental group, is not exposed to the **independent variables** under investigation; thus, in a clinical trial of a drug, control groups receive a **placebo** rather than the drug itself.

Control variable: A variable introduced to examine its impact on an existing association between an **independent variable** and a **dependent variable**.

Convenience sampling: A sample acquired with a minimum expenditure of resources, usually as part of a **pilot survey**.

Correlation: An index of the extent to which the values of two variables vary together with positive or negative values indicating the direction of the variation.

Covering letter: A letter that accompanies a questionnaire, setting out the nature and objectives of the research and designed to motivate the recipient to respond; also called a cover letter.

Covert research: Research involving deception and not based on the informed consent of its subjects.

Cross-tabulation: A joint **frequency distribution** of two or more variables in a row and column format (also called a **contingency table**).

Data file: The computer entity in which all the data collected in a survey are stored.

Data input: The entry of the appropriate code for a response from the **codebook** into a **data file**.

Dedicated application: Computer software designed to carry out a specialized function in connection with surveys (such as data analysis): see also **one-stop application**.

Dependent variable: A variable whose values are influenced by one or more **independent variables**.

Dichotomous: A variable which can have just two possible values, such as yes/no, true/false, 0/1.

Dispersion: Statistical measures (such as the range and standard deviation) that summarize a frequency distribution in terms of its variety or spread.

Disproportionate stratified sampling (DSS): A **stratified** random sample design in which a different sampling fraction is used for different strata.

Elaboration: A statistical procedure that examines the relationship between (usually) an **independent**, a **dependent** and a **control variable** by comparing the relationships between the first two in a series of **partial** sub-tables, one for each category of the control variable.

Empirical: Based on, or concerned with, observation and measurement.

Epidemiological (study, research): A type of research design, based on survey findings or the analysis of official statistics, that seeks to explain the distribution of death, illness, crime or deviance in a human population: the smoking and lung cancer research discussed in Box 1.4 is an example of epidemiology.

Epsem sample: A special sampling arrangement in which every case and every group of cases in the population stand an equal chance of inclusion in the **sample**.

Experiment: A research strategy in which the researcher aims to test hypotheses through a research design in which **independent variables** can be controlled and manipulated in order to measure their impact on a **dependent variable** or variables.

Experimental group: In an experimental design, a group which is exposed to the **independent variables** under investigation; thus, in a clinical trial of a drug, experimental groups receive the drug itself, not a **placebo**.

Frequency distribution: A table or chart summarizing the number of cases observed in each category of a **variable**.

General linear model (GLM): A statistical model on which several techniques of **multivariate analysis** are based.

Histogram: The graphical depiction of a **frequency distribution** in which bars represent the categories of a **continuous variable** with an **interval** or **ratio level of measurement**: the area of a bar is made proportional to the relative frequency of that category in the distribution.

Independent variable: A variable whose values have an effect on one or more **dependent variables**.

Interval level of measurement: See **levels of measurement**.

Interview guide: A list reminding the interviewer of the topics to be covered in an **unstructured interview**.

Interview schedule: A list of the questions to be asked by the interviewer, including instructions about procedures such as use of prompts and handling of queries and non-response.

Levels of measurement: The nature of the logical relations that exist between the categories employed in a **variable**, which dictates the statistical operations that can be performed on case values; progressively more sophisticated measurement can take place at each ascending level: in the lowest, **nominal**, level, the categories have no intrinsic ordering: in the **ordinal** level, they form a ranking: at the **interval** level, a unit of measurement enables the relative distance between cases in different categories to be established, while the **ratio** level identifies the absolute position of cases on the dimension concerned.

Likert scale: A question format, named after the American social psychologist, Rensis Likert, in which respondents indicate their agreement or disagreement with statements by choosing one of a set of categories ranging from, for example, strongly agree to strongly disagree.

Line (graph chart): A graphical representation of trends in the values of a variable or variables, plotting a time sequence from left to right on the x-axis of a graph.

Longitudinal survey: One which extends over a period of time, collecting the same data for different time periods; see also **panel study**.

Measures of association: Statistics designed to provide an indication of the strength of the relationship between two variables.

Multiple regression: A technique of **multivariate** analysis.

Multi-stage sampling: Designs in which the selection process is repeated several times with different sampling units, the cases selected at an earlier stage making up the **sampling frame** at the next stage.

Multivariate analysis: Statistical procedures concerned to examine the mutual influences that exist within a set of variables.

Nominal level of measurement: See **levels of measurement**.

Non-parametric statistics: Tests and measures which rest on relatively few assumptions about the population from which a sample is drawn.

Non-selection errors: Errors that affect surveys that have their origin outside the selection procedures (for example, mistakes by interviewers).

Null hypothesis: A statement that no difference exists between two samples or distributions that an investigator normally seeks to refute by conducting statistical tests on collected data.

One-stop (integrated) application: A software package that includes questionnaire design, data entry, data analysis and data presentation facilities.

Open-ended questions: Questions in which respondents are not offered alternative responses from which to choose, but are invited to give their answers in their own words; also called open questions.

Operationalization: The process of constructing empirical observations or measures that correspond to theoretical concepts.

Optical mark reader (OMR): An electronic method of processing respondents' answers to closed questions by scanning a pre-printed form for ticks or marks in designated areas.

Ordinal level of measurement: See **levels of measurement**.

Overt research: Research based on the informed consent of its subjects.

Panel study: Research in which similar data is repeatedly collected from the same respondents; see also **longitudinal survey**.

Partial: One of the sub-tables representing a value of a control variable created in the **elaboration** procedure.

Participant observation: A research technique, either **overt** or **covert**, in which the researcher observes a social collectivity of which she or he is a member, where membership is often only for the purposes of the research.

Pie chart: The graphical representation of a variable in which each segment of a circle represents a category; the area of each segment is proportional to the observed frequency and is usually labelled as a percentage; also called a pie diagram.

Piloting: Inclusive term for **pretests** and **pilot surveys**.

Pilot survey (project): A small-scale rehearsal of the survey proper, designed to test key features such as access to respondents, question wording, questionnaire layout, and arrangements for distribution and return of questionnaires.

Placebo: A harmless preparation that has no medical value or pharmacological effects, as given to the members of a **control group** in a clinical trial.

Population parameter: The value of a characteristic of the **target population** which the researcher may try to estimate using data derived from a **sample**.

Postal/mail questionnaire: A **self-completion questionnaire** sent to respondents by post or internal mail.

Post-coded: Variables, typically derived from **open-ended questions**, which are assigned categories and codes only after responses have been collected.

Precision: The average size of the difference between a **population parameter** and the estimates of it derived from all the possible samples of a given size and design selected from the **target population**.

Pre-coded: Variables, typically derived from **closed questions**, which are assigned codes prior to obtaining responses.

Pretest: A dummy run of part of the research instrument as an element in the **piloting**.

Primary sampling unit (PSU): The type of case that makes up the sampling frame in the first stage of a **multi-stage sampling** design.

Probability proportional to size (PPS): A technique in multi-stage sampling which seeks to control sample size by arranging for the chances of selection of sampling units to be proportional to their size.

Probability sampling: A method of drawing a **sample**, based on the mathematical theory of probability, that permits inferences to be made from it to the **target population**: a synonym for **random sampling**.

Probe: Any technique used by an interviewer to elicit a fuller response from an interviewee.

Prompt: A reminder to the respondent about the possible categories of response.

Proportional reduction in error measures (PRE): Measures based on the difference between attempting to predict the value of a dependent variable in complete ignorance and predicting it on the basis of the value of an observed independent variable.

Proportionate stratified sampling (PSS): A **stratified** random sample design in which the same (uniform) sampling fraction is used for all the strata.

Questionnaire: A research instrument consisting of a set of questions on a form which respondents fill in themselves; sometimes, though not in this book, used to include **interview schedules**, in which case the term **self-completion questionnaire** is normally used to distinguish it from the interview schedule.

Quota sampling: A technique in which interviewers are provided with a list of interlocking interviewee attributes, such as age and sex, which they can satisfy by selecting appropriate respondents.

Random assignment: In an experimental design, the random allocation of subjects to a **control group** or an **experimental group**.

Random sampling: See **probability sampling**.

Ratio level of measurement: See **levels of measurement**.

Reactivity of research instruments: The tendency for a measure to produce different results solely because it is being used by different researchers or in a different context; see also **reliability**.

Regression: An important family of multivariate techniques based on constructing equations with the dependent variable on one side and independent variables, coefficients of association and an error term on the other.

Reliability: The extent to which a measuring instrument, such as a test or indicator, consistently produces the same results when used in the same conditions; see also **validity**.

Residual: A term in a regression equation that represents the variation in the dependent variable that remains unaccounted for.

Response bias: A predisposition amongst respondents to answer questions in a particular fashion irrespective of their content (for example, an acquiescence bias is a general tendency to agree with statements and answer yes to items): see also **social desirability**.

Response processing: The operations involved in converting respondents' answers into a digital format that can be handled by a computer survey analysis package.

Response rate: The proportion of respondents who produce a usable set of responses out of the total number in the **sample**.

Salience: The importance of an issue to a respondent.

Sample: The sub-set of cases selected from the **target population** from which an attempt is made to collect data.

Sampling distribution: Theoretical distributions which correspond to the results from random samples repeatedly drawn from populations: the *normal distribution* and *student's t* are two widely used sampling distributions.

Sampling error: Different random samples of the same size and design will contain different cases and thus generate different estimates of **population parameters**: sampling error is the average spread between such estimates, and is measured by the **standard error** family of statistics.

Sampling frame: A listing of every case in the **target population**.

Sampling interval (sampling fraction): The interval between the cases selected for the sample on a **sampling frame** (calculated by dividing the size of the population by the size of the desired sample).

Sampling unit: An element in terms of which a **target population** is organized for **multi-stage sampling**: the general public in the UK could be thought of as organized into *administrative regions, parliamentary constituencies, boroughs, wards, street addresses,* and *households*: the first element in a multi-stage design is the **primary sampling unit**.

Scientific sampling: An alternative term for **probability sampling**.

Selection errors: Errors in surveys that have their origin in some aspect of the sample selection procedures (for example, **sampling error**).

Self-completion questionnaire: A form filled in by the respondent in contrast to an **interview schedule** completed by an interviewer.

Semantic differential: A question format in which respondents are asked to rate items on a bipolar scale, where the poles (extremes) of the scale are described by a pair of adjectives such as warm/cold, strong/weak and so on.

Semi-structured interview: An interviewer employs a list of topics, possibly in a prescribed order, but not a complete script.

Show card: A list of response categories shown to a respondent; a form of **prompt**.

Simple random sampling (SRS): A basic sampling design based on a single stage of selection from a sampling frame representing the whole of the **target population**.

Snowball sampling: A procedure in which a few early cases located by researchers are used as the source of all the further cases in the **sample**.

Social desirability: A **reactivity** problem, specifically a **response bias** produced by the tendency of respondents to give socially approved answers, or to engage in socially approved behaviour when observed by a researcher.

Standard error: A statistical measure of the level of **precision** of the values generated in the estimation process: each kind of descriptive and summary statistic has its own measure of precision, for example, standard error of the mean, standard error of the percentage, etc.

Standardized variables (Z scores): The transformation of the observed values of a variable so that it is numerically comparable to other variables: the resulting values have a mean of zero and a standard deviation of 1.

Statistical inference: The attempt to predict population values based on sample data.

Statistical Package for the Social Sciences (SPSS): A widely used, **dedicated** computer application for the analysis of survey data.

Statistical significance: A measure of how likely it is that an observed difference is due entirely to sampling variations.

Stem and leaf plot: A graphical way of displaying a **frequency distribution**.

Stratified sampling: A refinement to **simple random sampling** in which the cases in the **target population** are divided into separate strata or groupings on the basis of a characteristic relevant to the research, with subsequent selection taking place from each stratum separately.

Structured interview: An interview in which the precise wording and sequence of questions are predetermined by the researcher.

Survey: A research strategy in which the same information about all the **cases** in a **sample** is systematically collected in a standardized form.

Survey fatigue: A general tendency for response rates to decline as respondents grow weary of repeated social surveys.

Symmetry: Statistical measures (such as skew and kurtosis) that summarize a **frequency distribution** in terms of its overall shape.

Systematic selection: A procedure for selecting cases for the **sample** at a chosen period or **sampling interval** within the **sampling frame**, for example, choosing every tenth case.

Taking the role of the other: A conscious attempt by a researcher or other actor to recognize the situation and outlook of another individual.

Target population: The pool of cases relevant to a research topic from which a **sample** is selected.

Theoretical: Based on abstraction and idealization and concerned with explanation and prediction.

Theoretical population: The infinite set of populations to which any general theory relates.

Theoretical sampling: A component of *grounded theory* strategies in which cases are selected for their theoretically significant attributes rather than for their typicality.

Time-series: Data derived from a **longitudinal survey** or **panel study.**

Triangulation: Use of a variety of research strategies, or of data from a variety of sources, to test an hypothesis.

Unstructured interview: An interview in which neither the precise wording nor the sequence of questions are predetermined by the researcher.

Validity: Whether a measuring instrument, such as a test or indicator, succeeds in measuring what it was designed for; see also **reliability.**

Variable: A characteristic that is fixed at any one point of time for any **case** but varies between cases.

Vignette: A constructed story presented to respondents in order to elicit an account of what they think should be done or what they would do themselves in such a situation.

Z scores: See **standardized variables.**

Appendix 1:
The *Travel Survey* questionnaires

Staff Campus Travel Survey 1998

This questionnaire has been sent to a sample selected at random from all main campus staff. It is entirely anonymous. Further details of the objectives and the prize draw for respondents are supplied on the covering letter. Please reply using the internal post to the Survey Unit, C51 Portland Building, by May 12th.

1 What is the approximate distance from your home to your workplace?

Please ✓ one box

Less than one mile	☐ 1
1 or 2 miles	☐ 2
3 or 4 miles	☐ 3
5 or 6 miles	☐ 4
7 to 9 miles	☐ 5
10 to 19 miles	☐ 6
20 or more miles	☐ 7

2 Approximately how long does it take you on average to travel to work?

Please ✓ one box

Less than 15 minutes	☐ 1
15-29 minutes	☐ 2
30-44 minutes	☐ 3
45-59 minutes	☐ 4
60-89 minutes	☐ 5
90 minutes or more	☐ 6

3 Which mode of transport do you use most often for the longest stage of your journey to work?

Please ✓ one box

Walk	☐ 1
Bicycle	☐ 2
Rail	☐ 3
Bus	☐ 4
Car as driver	☐ 5
Car as passenger	☐ 6
Motorbike as driver	☐ 7
Motorbike as passenger	☐ 8

4 Do you use once a week, or more frequently, any alternative modes of transport for part or all of your journey to work?

Please ✓ all that apply

No regular alternatives	☐ 1
Walk	☐ 2
Bicycle	☐ 3
Rail	☐ 4
Bus	☐ 5
Car as driver	☐ 6
Car as passenger	☐ 7
Motorbike as driver	☐ 8
Motorbike as passenger	☐ 9

5 On occasions when you travel to the campus by car, where do you park?

Please ✓ one box

Not applicable	☐ 1
In the Science City area	☐ 2
In the central area (including Highfields House, West Drive and Education)	☐ 3
On the periphery (Including Halls, History and the Sports Centre)	☐ 4

6 How often do you travel off the campus for work-related purposes?

Please ✓ one box

5 days a week or more	☐ 1
3 or 4 days a week	☐ 2
Once or twice a week	☐ 3
Less than once a week	☐ 4
Never	☐ 5 → **Please go to Question 8**

7 What mode of travel do you use most frequently for the journeys covered by question 6?

Please ✓ one box

Walk	☐ 1
Bicycle	☐ 2
Rail	☐ 3
Bus	☐ 4
Car as driver	☐ 5
Car as passenger	☐ 6
Motorbike as driver	☐ 7
Motorbike as passenger	☐ 8

Question 8 is for those who WALK part or all of their journey to work once a week or more

8 How do you think facilities for pedestrians could be improved?

_____
_____
_____
_____

Question 9 is for those who CYCLE for part or all of their journey to work once a week or more

9 How do you think facilities for cyclists could be improved?

_____
_____
_____
_____

Questions 10, 11 & 12 are for those who use PUBLIC TRANSPORT for part or all of their journey to work once a week or more

10 Do you purchase season tickets for bus/rail travel to the campus? Yes ☐ 1 No ☐ 2

11 Please indicate your daily return fare in the boxes. If you have a season ticket please apportion the total cost on a daily basis.

£ £ p p

12 How do you think facilities for public transport users could be improved?

_____
_____
_____
_____

Questions 13 & 14 are for those who use a CAR for their journey from home to work once a week or more. If you do not use a car, please go to Question 15.

13 How important are the following considerations in your decision to use a car to travel to work?

	An important consideration	Of some importance	Not important
Speed of car journeys	☐1	☐2	☐3
Flexibility and convenience	☐1	☐2	☐3
High cost of public transport	☐1	☐2	☐3
Safety and security	☐1	☐2	☐3
No direct bus service to campus	☐1	☐2	☐3
Lack of cycle facilities	☐1	☐2	☐3

If there are any other important considerations for you not mentioned above, please describe them here.

_____
_____
_____
_____
_____
_____
_____
_____
_____
_____
_____
_____
_____
_____
_____
_____
_____
_____

14 How likely would the following developments be to alter the way you travel to work?

	Very likely	Possibly	Unlikely
Subsidised travel cards for public transport	☐1	☐2	☐3
More direct bus routes to campus	☐1	☐2	☐3
Campus car park charging	☐1	☐2	☐3
Improved shower facilities in your building	☐1	☐2	☐3
Improved cycle security	☐1	☐2	☐3

This final section seeks background information necessary for us to interpret your other responses. May we reassure you that under no circumstances will attempts be made to identify individuals.

15 At what time do you usually arrive at work?

Please ✓ one box

Before 06.00	☐1	09.30 - 12.29	☐2
06.00 - 07.59	☐3	12.30 - 17:30	☐4
08.00 - 08.29	☐5	After 17.30	☐6
08.30 - 08.59	☐7	No regular time of arrival	☐8
09.00 - 09.29	☐9		

16 Do you work shifts or a rota system?

Yes ☐1   No ☐2

17 Do you have a part-time contract?

Yes ☐1   No ☐2

18 How many days per week do you visit the campus?

☐ days per week

19 To which one of the following staff categories do you belong?

Academic	☐1	Academic related	☐2
Secretarial, Clerical & Junior Administrative	☐3	Technical	☐4
Manual & Ancillary	☐5	Other (please specify)	

_____

20 In what part of the University system do you work?

Arts	☐01	Registrar's	☐02
Law & Social Sciences	☐03	Bursar's	☐04
Education	☐05	Libraries	☐06
Science	☐07	Computing Centre	☐08
Engineering	☐09	Other (please specify)	
Medicine	☐10		

_____

21 What is the postcode of your home address?

22 What is the total number of cars and motorbikes that are available to your household?

None ☐1   One ☐2   More than one ☐3

23 How attractive for you personally is the prospect of working from home for at least part of the week?

None of my job could be done from home	☐1
Don't know / I would need to think about it	☐2
An unattractive prospect	☐3
A fairly attractive prospect	☐4
A very attractive prospect	☐5
I already work from home	☐6

Thank you for taking the time to complete this questionnaire. Please return it in the INTERNAL mail using the envelope provided.

Student Campus Travel Survey 1998

This questionnaire has been sent to a sample selected at random from all main campus students. It is entirely anonymous. Further details of the objectives and the prize draw for respondents are supplied on the covering letter. Please reply using the internal post to the Survey Unit, C51 Portland Building, by May 12th.

1 What is the approximate distance from your Nottingham address to where your teaching and/or research normally takes place?

Please ✓ one box

Less than one mile	☐1
1 or 2 miles	☐2
3 or 4 miles	☐3
5 or 6 miles	☐4
7 to 9 miles	☐5
10 to 19 miles	☐6
20 or more miles	☐7

2 Approximately how long does it take you on average to travel from your Nottingham address to where your teaching or research normally takes place?

Please ✓ one box

Less than 15 minutes	☐1
15-29 minutes	☐2
30-44 minutes	☐3
45-59 minutes	☐4
60-89 minutes	☐5
90 minutes or more	☐6

3 Which mode of transport do you use most often for the longest stage of your journey to the campus?

Please ✓ one box

Walk	☐1
Bicycle	☐2
Rail	☐3
Bus	☐4
Car as driver	☐5
Car as passenger	☐6
Motorbike as driver	☐7
Motorbike as passenger	☐8

4 Do you use once a week, or more frequently, any alternative modes of transport for part or all of your journey to the campus?

Please ✓ all that apply

No regular alternatives	☐1
Walk	☐2
Bicycle	☐3
Rail	☐4
Bus	☐5
Car as driver	☐6
Car as passenger	☐7
Motorbike as driver	☐8
Motorbike as passenger	☐9

5 On occasions when you travel to the campus by car, where do you park?

Please ✓ one box

Not applicable	☐1
In the Science City area	☐2
In the central area (including Highfields House, West Drive and Education)	☐3
On the periphery (Including Halls, History and the Sports Centre)	☐4
Elsewhere	☐5

6 How often do you travel off the campus and return later on the same day?

Please ✓ one box

5 days a week or more	☐1
3 or 4 days a week	☐2
Once or twice a week	☐3
Less than once a week	☐4
Never	☐5 ➤ **Please go to Question 8**

7 What mode of travel do you use most frequently for the journeys covered by question 6?

Please ✓ one box

Walk	☐1
Bicycle	☐2
Rail	☐3
Bus	☐4
Car as driver	☐5
Car as passenger	☐6
Motorbike as driver	☐7
Motorbike as passenger	☐8

Question 8 is for those who WALK part or all of their journey to the campus once a week or more

8 How do you think facilities for pedestrians could be improved?

_____
_____
_____
_____
_____

Question 9 is for those who CYCLE for part or all of their journey to the campus once a week or more

9 How do you think facilities for cyclists could be improved?

_____
_____
_____
_____
_____

Questions 10, 11 & 12 are for those who use PUBLIC TRANSPORT for part or all of their journey to the campus once a week or more

10 Do you purchase season tickets for bus/rail travel to the campus?   Yes ☐1   No ☐2

11 Please indicate your daily return fare in the boxes. If you have a season ticket please apportion the total cost on a daily basis.

£ £ p p

12 How do you think facilities for public transport users could be improved?

_____
_____
_____
_____
_____

Questions 13 & 14 are for those who use a CAR for their journey from their term time address to the campus once a week or more. If you do not use a car, please go to Question 15.

13 How important are the following considerations in your decision to use a car to travel to the campus?

	An important consideration	Of some importance	Not important
Speed of car journeys	☐1	☐2	☐3
Flexibility and convenience	☐1	☐2	☐3
High cost of public transport	☐1	☐2	☐3
Safety and security	☐1	☐2	☐3
No direct bus service to campus	☐1	☐2	☐3
Lack of cycle facilities	☐1	☐2	☐3

If there are any other important considerations for you not mentioned above, please describe them here.

_____
_____
_____
_____
_____
_____
_____
_____
_____
_____
_____
_____
_____
_____
_____
_____
_____
_____
_____

14 How likely would the following developments be to alter the way you travel to the campus?

	Very likely	Possibly	Unlikely
Subsidised travel cards for public transport	☐1	☐2	☐3
More direct bus routes to campus	☐1	☐2	☐3
Campus car park charging	☐1	☐2	☐3
Improved shower facilities in your building	☐1	☐2	☐3
Improved cycle security	☐1	☐2	☐3

This final section seeks background information necessary for us to interpret your other responses. May we reassure you that under no circumstances will attempts be made to identify individuals.

15 At what time do you usually arrive on campus?

Please ✓ one box

Before 06.00	☐1	09.30 - 12.29	☐2
06.00 - 07.59	☐3	12.30 - 17:30	☐4
08.00 - 08.29	☐5	After 17.30	☐6
08.30 - 08.59	☐7	No regular time of arrival	☐8
09.00 - 09.29	☐9		

16 How many days per week do you visit the campus?

☐ days per week

17 Which of the following are you?

Please ✓ one box

Full-time undergraduate ☐1
Full-time postgraduate ☐2
Part-time undergraduate ☐3
Part-time postgraduate ☐4

18 Which Faculty are you in?

Please ✓ one box

Arts ☐1
Law & Social Science ☐2
Education ☐3
Science ☐4
Engineering ☐5
Medicine ☐6

19 What is the postcode of your Nottingham address?

20 What is the total number of cars and motorbikes that are available for your use as a driver or passenger within your household?

None ☐1 One ☐2 More than one ☐3

21 The following space is available for any other comments you would like to make about travel to, across and from the campus.

_____
_____
_____
_____
_____
_____
_____
_____
_____
_____
_____
_____

Thank you for taking the time to complete this questionnaire. Please return it in the INTERNAL mail using the envelope provided.

Appendix 2: Websites of professional associations

Many professional associations of academic researchers and teachers publish codes of professional conduct, including ethical guidance on the conduct of research. These guidelines are accessible through the world wide web. Here is a selection of some that are particularly relevant to survey research.

British Sociological Association
   Home page: www.britsoc.org.uk/

American Sociological Association
   Home page: www.asanet.org/

British Psychological Society
   Home page: www.bps.org.uk/

The Australian Sociological Association
   Home page: www.newcastle.edu.au/department/so/tasa/

Sociological Association of Aotearoa (New Zealand)
   Home page: saanz.science.org.nz/

Canadian Sociology and Anthropology Association
   Home page: www.arts.ubc.ca/csaa/

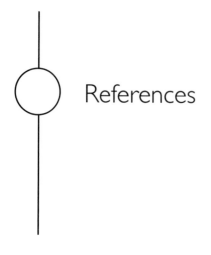

References

Abercrombie, N., Baker, J., Brett, S. and Foster, J. (1970) Superstition and religion: the God of the gaps, in D. Martin and M. Hill (eds) *A Sociological Yearbook of Religion in Britain*, Volume 3. London: SCM.

Alasuutari, P. (1995) *Researching Culture: Qualitative Method and Cultural Studies*. London: Sage.

Aldridge, A. E. (2000) *Religion in the Contemporary World: A Sociological Introduction*. Cambridge: Polity.

Babbie, E. R. (2001) *The Practice of Social Research*, 9th edn. Belmont, CA: Wadsworth.

Barker, E. (1984) *The Making of a Moonie: Choice or Brainwashing?* Oxford: Blackwell.

Barnett, V. (1991) *Sample Survey Principles and Methods*. London: Edward Arnold.

Beck, A. T., Brown, G., Epstein, N. and Steer, R. A. (1988) An inventory for measuring clinical anxiety: psychometric properties, *Journal of Consulting and Clinical Psychology*, 56: 893–7.

Bennett, N. with Jordan, J., Long, G. and Wade, B. (1976) *Teaching Styles and Pupil Progress*. London: Open Books Publishing.

Blumer, H. (1956) Sociological analysis and the 'variable', *American Sociological Review*, 21: 683–90.

Booth, C. (1889–1902) *Life and Labour of the People in London*. London: Macmillan.

Bourque, L. B. and Fielder, E. P. (1995) *How to Conduct Self-administered and Mail Surveys*. Thousand Oaks, CA: Sage.

Bowley, A. L. and Burnett-Hurst, A. (1915) *Livelihood and Poverty*. London: Ratan Tata Foundation, University of London.

Bryman, A. and Cramer, D. (1990) *Quantitative Data Analysis for Social Scientists.* London: Routledge.

Buchanan, D., Boddy, D. and McCalman, J. (1988) Getting in, getting on, getting out, and getting back, in A. Bryman (ed.) *Doing Research in Organizations.* London: Routledge.

Chalmers, A. F. (1999) *What is This Thing called Science?*, 3rd edn. Buckingham: Open University Press.

Cohen, A. K. (1955) *Delinquent Boys: The Culture of the Gang.* New York: Free Press.

Coleman, C. and Moynihan, J. (1996) *Understanding Crime Data.* Buckingham: Open University Press.

Cutts, M. (1996) *The Plain English Guide.* Oxford: Oxford University Press.

Czaja, R. and Blair, J. (1995) *Designing Surveys: A Guide to Decisions and Procedures.* Thousand Oaks, CA: Sage.

Davie, D. (1988) *To Scorch or Freeze: Poems About the Sacred.* Manchester: Carcanet.

de Vaus, D. A. (1991) *Surveys in Social Research*, 3rd edn. London: UCL Press.

Devine, F. and Heath, S. (1999) *Sociological Research Methods in Context.* London: Macmillan.

Doll, R. and Hill, A. B. (1952) A study of the aetiology of carcinoma of the lung, *British Medical Journal*, 13 December: 1271–85.

Doll, R. and Peto, R. (1976) Mortality in relation to smoking: 20 years' observations of male British doctors, *British Medical Journal*, 25 December: 1525–36.

ESRC (Economic and Social Research Council) (1995) *Writing for Business: How to Write Reports that Capture the Attention of Businesses.* Swindon: ESRC.

Evans, H. (2000) *Essential English for Journalists, Editors and Writers.* London: Pimlico.

Everitt, B. S. and Dunn, G. (1991) *Applied Multivariate Analysis.* London: Edward Arnold.

Fielding, J. and Gilbert, N. (1999) *Understanding Social Statistics.* London: Sage.

Finch, J. and Mason, J. (1993) *Negotiating Family Responsibilities.* London: Routledge.

Fink, A. (ed.) (1995) *The Survey Handbook.* Thousand Oaks, CA: Sage.

Gilbert, N. (1993a) Writing about social research, in N. Gilbert (ed.) *Researching Social Life.* London: Sage.

Gilbert, N. (1993b) *Analysing Tabular Data: Loglinear and Logistic Models for Social Researchers.* London: UCL Press.

Glaser, B. G. and Strauss, A. L. (1967) *The Discovery of Grounded Theory: Strategies for Qualitative Research.* New York: Aldine.

Goldthorpe, J. H., Lockwood, D., Bechhofer, F. and Platt, J. (1969) *The Affluent Worker in the Class Structure.* Cambridge: Cambridge University Press.

Hammond, P. E. (ed.) (1964) *Sociologists at Work: Essays on the Craft of Social Research.* New York: Basic Books.

Healey, J. F. (1990) *Statistics: A Tool for Social Research.* Belmont, CA: Wadsworth.

Hornsby-Smith, M. (1993) Gaining access, in N. Gilbert (ed.) *Researching Social Life.* London: Sage.

Hughes, J. A. (1976) *Sociological Analysis: Methods of Discovery.* London: Nelson.

Hughes, J. A. and Sharrock, W. (1997) *The Philosophy of Social Research*, 3rd edn London: Longman.

Kalton, G. (1966) *An Introduction to Statistical Ideas for Social Scientists*. London: Chapman and Hall.

Kalton, G. (1983) *Introduction to Survey Sampling*. London: Sage.

Kish, L. (1965) *Survey Sampling*. New York: Wiley.

Lazarsfeld, P. (1958) Evidence and inference in social research, *Daedalus*, 87: 99–130.

Levine, K. (1999) Definitional and methodological problems in the cross-national measurement of adult literacy, *Written Language and Literacy*, 1(1): 41–62.

Litwin, M. S. (1995) *How to Measure Survey Reliability and Validity*. Thousand Oaks, CA: Sage.

Loether, H. J. and McTavish, D. G. (1974) *Descriptive Statistics for Sociologists*. Boston: Allyn and Bacon.

Marsh, C. (1982) *The Survey Method: The Contribution of Surveys to Sociological Explanation*. London: George Allen and Unwin.

Marsh, C. (1988) *Exploring Data: An Introduction to Data Analysis for Social Scientists*. Cambridge: Polity.

Miller, D. E. (1991) *Handbook of Research Design and Social Measurement*, 5th edn. London: Longman.

Mills, C. Wright (1970) *The Sociological Imagination*. Harmondsworth: Penguin.

Moser, C. A. and Kalton, G. (1971) *Survey Methods in Social Investigation*, 2nd edn. London: Heinemann Educational Books.

Murphy, L. L., Conoley, J. C. and Impara, J. C. (eds) (1994) *Tests in Print* (IV): *An Index to Tests, Test Reviews and the Literature on Specific Tests*. Lincoln, Nebraska: Buros Institute of Mental Measurements.

Norusis, M. J. (1995) *SPSS 6.1: Guide to Data Analysis*. Englewood Cliffs, CA: Prentice Hall.

Oakley, A. (1998) Gender, methodology and people's ways of knowing: some problems with feminism and the paradigm debate is social science, *Sociology*, 32(4): 707–31.

OECD (1995) *Literacy, Economy and Society: Results of the First International Adult Literacy Survey*. Paris: Organization for Economic Co-operation and Development.

OPCS (1991) *Standard Occupational Classification. Volume 3*. London: HMSO.

Oppenheim, A. N. (1992) *Questionnaire Design, Interviewing and Attitude Measurement*. London: Pinter.

Robson, C. (1993) *Real World Research*. Oxford: Blackwell.

Rose, D. and Sullivan, O. (1996) *Introducing Data Analysis for Social Scientists*, 2nd edn. Buckingham: Open University Press.

Rose, D. and O'Reilly, K. (eds) (1997) *Constructing Classes: Towards a New Social Classification for the UK*. Swindon: ESRC/ONS.

Rowntree, B. Seebohm (1902) *Poverty: A Study of Town Life*. London: Macmillan.

Saunders, P. (1990) *A Nation of Home Owners*. London: Unwin Hyman.

Siegel, S. and Castellan, N. J. Jr. (1988) *Non-parametric Statistics for the Behavioural Sciences*, 2nd edn. New York: McGraw-Hill.

Strauss, A. L. (1987) *Qualitative Analysis for Social Scientists*. Cambridge: Cambridge University Press.

Strauss, A. L. and Corbin, J. (1993) *Basics of Qualitative Research: Grounded Theory Procedures and Techniques.* Newbury Park: Sage.

Titmuss, R. M. (1970) *The Gift Relationship: From Human Blood to Social Policy.* London: Allen & Unwin.

Webster, F. (1995) *Theories of the Information Society.* London: Routledge.

Wright, E. O. (1985) *Classes.* London: Verso.

Zigmond, A. and Snaith, R. (1983) The Hospital Anxiety and Depression Scale, *Acta Psychiatrica Scandinavica*, 67: 361–70.

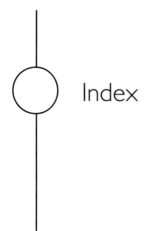

Index